Nancy Opel and Robert Stanton in a scene from "Sure Thing" from the Primary Stages production of "All in the Timing." Set design by Bruce Goodrich.

ALL IN THE TIMING

Six One-Act Comedies

BY DAVID IVES

★

★

DRAMATISTS
PLAY SERVICE
INC.

SPECIAL NOTE

Anyone receiving permission to produce any or all of the Plays in the volume ALL IN THE TIMING: Six One-Act Comedies is required to give credit to the Author as sole and exclusive Author of the Play(s) on the title page of all programs distributed in connection with performances of the Play(s) and in all instances in which the title(s) of the Play(s) appears for purposes of advertising, publicizing or otherwise exploiting the Play(s) and/or a production thereof. The name of the Author must appear on a separate line, in which no other name appears, immediately beneath the title(s) and in size of type equal to 50% of the size of the largest, most prominent letter used for the title(s) of the Play(s). No person, firm or entity may receive credit larger or more prominent than that accorded the Author. The following acknowledgment(s) must appear on the title page in all programs distributed in connection with performances of the Play(s):

WORDS, WORDS, WORDS was first produced at the
Manhattan Punch Line Theatre in New York City, in January 1987,
Steve Kaplan, Artistic Director

SURE THING was first produced at the
Manhattan Punch Line Theatre in New York City, in February 1988,
Steve Kaplan, Artistic Director.

PHILIP GLASS BUYS A LOAF OF BREAD was first produced at the
Manhattan Punch Line Theatre in New York City, in January 1990,
Steve Kaplan, Artistic Director.

VARIATIONS ON THE DEATH OF TROTSKY was first produced at the
Manhattan Punch Line Theatre in New York City, in January 1991,
Steve Kaplan, Artistic Director.

THE PHILADELPHIA was first produced at the
1992 New Hope Performing Arts Festival, presented by
The New Hope Arts Commission, New Hope, Pennsylvania,
Robin Larsen, Executive Director.

THE UNIVERSAL LANGUAGE was first produced
by Primary Stages Company in New York City, in November 1993,
Casey Childs, Artistic Director.

ALL IN THE TIMING

Six One-Act Comedies

TABLE OF CONTENTS

SURE THING

This play is for Jason Buzas

SURE THING was presented as part of ALL IN THE TIMING at Primary Stages (Casey Childs, Artistic Director), in New York City, in December, 1993. It was directed by Jason McConnell Buzas; the set design was by Bruce Goodrich; the costume design was by Sharon Lynch; the lighting design was by Deborah Constantine and the production stage manager was Christine Catti. The cast was as follows:

BILL.. Robert Stanton
BETTY .... Nancy Opel

SURE THING premiered at the Manhattan Punch Line Theatre, in New York City, in February 1988. It was directed by Jason McConnell Buzas; the set design was by Stanley A. Meyer; the costume design was by Michael S. Schler; the lighting design was by Joseph R. Morley; the sound design was by Duncan Edwards and the stage manager was Carl Gonzalez. The cast was as follows:

BILL.. Robert Stanton
BETTY .... Nancy Opel

CHARACTERS

BILL and BETTY, both in their late 20s

SETTING

A café table, with a couple of chairs

IMPORTANT NOTE

The bell is not visible, is not onstage, is not on the table or anywhere else in sight. It is rung from the wings and neither Bill nor Betty ever acknowledges the sound of the bell.

SURE THING

Betty is reading at the table. An empty chair opposite her. Bill enters.

BILL. Excuse me. Is this chair taken?

BETTY. Excuse me?

BILL. Is this taken?

BETTY. Yes it is.

BILL. Oh. Sorry.

BETTY. Sure thing. *(A bell rings softly.)*

BILL. Excuse me. Is this chair taken?

BETTY. Excuse me?

BILL. Is this taken?

BETTY. No, but I'm expecting somebody in a minute.

BILL. Oh. Thanks anyway.

BETTY. Sure thing. *(A bell rings softly.)*

BILL. Excuse me. Is this chair taken?

BETTY. No, but I'm expecting somebody very shortly.

BILL. Would you mind if I sit here till he or she or it comes?

BETTY. *(Glances at her watch.)* They do seem to be pretty late ...

BILL. You never know who you might be turning down.

BETTY. Sorry. Nice try, though.

BILL. Sure thing. *(Bell.)* Is this seat taken?

BETTY. No it's not.

BILL. Would you mind if I sit here?

BETTY. Yes I would.

BILL. Oh. *(Bell.)* Is this chair taken?

BETTY. No it's not.

BILL. Would you mind if I sit here?

BETTY. No. Go ahead.

BILL. Thanks. *(He sits. She continues reading.)* Every place else seems to be taken.

BETTY.   Mm-hm.

BILL.   Great place.

BETTY.   Mm-hm.

BILL. What's the book?

BETTY.   I just wanted to read in quiet, if you don't mind.

BILL.   No. Sure thing. *(Bell.)* Every place else seems to be taken.

BETTY.   Mm-hm.

BILL.   Great place for reading.

BETTY.   Yes, I like it.

BILL.   What's the book?

BETTY.   *The Sound and the Fury.*

BILL.   Oh. Hemingway. *(Bell.)* What's the book?

BETTY.   *The Sound and the Fury.*

BILL.   Oh. Faulkner.

BETTY.   Have you read it?

BILL.   Not ... actually. I've sure read *about* it, though. It's supposed to be great.

BETTY.   It is great.

BILL.   I hear it's great. *(Small pause.)* Waiter? *(Bell.)* What's the book?

BETTY.   *The Sound and the Fury.*

BILL.   Oh. Faulkner.

BETTY.   Have you read it?

BILL.   I'm a Mets fan, myself. *(Bell.)*

BETTY.   Have you read it?

BILL.   Yeah, I read it in college.

BETTY.   Where was college?

BILL.   I went to Oral Roberts University. *(Bell.)*

BETTY.   Where was college?

BILL.   I was lying. I never really went to college. I just like to party. *(Bell.)*

BETTY.   Where was college?

BILL.   Harvard.

BETTY.   Do you like Faulkner?

BILL.   I love Faulkner. I spent a whole winter reading him once.

BETTY. I've just started.

BILL. I was so excited after ten pages that I went out and bought everything else he wrote. One of the greatest reading experiences of my life. I mean, all that incredible psychological understanding. Page after page of gorgeous prose. His profound grasp of the mystery of time and human existence. The smells of the earth.... What do you think?

BETTY. I think it's pretty boring. (*Bell.*)

BILL. What's the book?

BETTY. *The Sound and the Fury.*

BILL. Oh! Faulkner!

BETTY. Do you like Faulkner?

BILL. I love Faulkner.

BETTY. He's incredible.

BILL. I spent a whole winter reading him once.

BETTY. I was so excited after ten pages that I went out and bought everything else he wrote.

BILL. All that incredible psychological understanding.

BETTY. And the prose is so gorgeous.

BILL. And the way he's grasped the mystery of time —

BETTY. — and human existence. I can't believe I've waited this long to read him.

BILL. You never know. You might not have liked him before.

BETTY. That's true.

BILL. You might not have been ready for him. You have to hit these things at the right moment or it's no good.

BETTY. That's happened to me.

BILL. It's all in the timing. (*Small pause.*) My name's Bill, by the way.

BETTY. I'm Betty.

BILL. Hi.

BETTY. Hi. (*Small pause.*)

BILL. Yes I thought reading Faulkner was ... a great experience.

BETTY. Yes. (*Small pause.*)

BILL. *The Sound and the Fury* ... (*Another small pause.*)

BETTY. Well. Onwards and upwards. (*She goes back to her*

book.)

BILL.   Waiter—? *(Bell.)* You have to hit these things at the right moment or it's no good.

BETTY.   That's happened to me.

BILL.   It's all in the timing. My name's Bill, by the way.

BETTY.   I'm Betty.

BILL.   Hi.

BETTY.   Hi.

BILL.   Do you come in here a lot?

BETTY.   Actually I'm just in town for two days from Pakistan.

BILL.   Oh. Pakistan. *(Bell.)* My name's Bill, by the way.

BETTY.   I'm Betty.

BILL.   Hi.

BETTY.   Hi.

BILL.   Do you come in here a lot?

BETTY.   Every once in a while. Do you?

BILL.   Not so much anymore. Not as much as I used to. Before my nervous breakdown. *(Bell.)* Do you come in here a lot?

BETTY.   Why are you asking?

BILL.   Just interested.

BETTY.   Are you really interested, or do you just want to pick me up?

BILL.   No, I'm really interested.

BETTY.   Why would you be interested in whether I come in here a lot?

BILL.   Just ... getting acquainted.

BETTY.   Maybe you're only interested for the sake of making small talk long enough to ask me back to your place to listen to some music, or because you've just rented some great tape for your VCR, or because you've got some terrific unknown Django Reinhardt record, only all you really want to do is fuck — which you won't do very well — after which you'll go into the bathroom and pee very loudly, then pad into the kitchen and get yourself a beer from the refrigerator without asking me whether I'd like anything, and then you'll proceed to lie back down beside me and confess that you've got a girlfriend named Stephanie who's away at medical school in Belgium for a year, and that you've been involved

16

with her — *off and on* — in what you'll call a very "intricate" relationship, for about *seven YEARS*. None of which *interests* me, mister!

BILL.   Okay. *(Bell.)* Do you come in here a lot?

BETTY.   Every other day, I think.

BILL.   I come in here quite a lot and I don't remember seeing you.

BETTY.   I guess we must be on different schedules.

BILL.   Missed connections.

BETTY.   Yes. Different time zones.

BILL.   Amazing how you can live right next door to somebody in this town and never even know it.

BETTY.   I know.

BILL.   City life.

BETTY.   It's crazy.

BILL.   We probably pass each other in the street every day. Right in front of this place, probably.

BETTY.   Yep.

BILL.   *(Looks around.)* Well the waiters here sure seem to be in some different time zone. I can't seem to locate one anywhere.... Waiter! *(He looks back.)* So what do you — *(He sees that she's gone back to her book.)*

BETTY.   I beg pardon?

BILL.   Nothing. Sorry. *(Bell.)*

BETTY.   I guess we must be on different schedules.

BILL.   Missed connections.

BETTY.   Yes. Different time zones.

BILL.   Amazing how you can live right next door to somebody in this town and never even know it.

BETTY.   I know.

BILL.   City life.

BETTY.   It's crazy.

BILL.   You weren't waiting for somebody when I came in, were you?

BETTY.   Actually I was.

BILL.   Oh. Boyfriend?

BETTY.   Sort of.

BILL.   What's a sort-of boyfriend?

17

BETTY.   My husband.

BILL.   Ah-ha. *(Bell.)* You weren't waiting for somebody when I came in, were you?

BETTY.   Actually I was.

BILL.   Oh. Boyfriend?

BETTY.   Sort of.

BILL.   What's a sort-of boyfriend?

BETTY.   We were meeting here to break up.

BILL.   Mm-hm ... *(Bell.)* What's a sort-of boyfriend?

BETTY.   My lover. Here she comes right now! *(Bell.)*

BILL.   You weren't waiting for somebody when I came in, were you?

BETTY.   No, just reading.

BILL.   Sort of a sad occupation for a Friday night, isn't it? Reading here, all by yourself?

BETTY.   Do you think so?

BILL.   Well sure. I mean, what's a good-looking woman like you doing out alone on a Friday night?

BETTY.   Trying to keep away from lines like that.

BILL. No, listen — *(Bell.)* You weren't waiting for somebody when I came in, were you?

BETTY.   No, just reading.

BILL.   Sort of a sad occupation for a Friday night, isn't it? Reading here all by yourself?

BETTY.   I guess it is, in a way.

BILL.   What's a good-looking woman like you doing out alone on a Friday night anyway? No offense, but ...

BETTY.   I'm out alone on a Friday night for the first time in a very long time.

BILL.   Oh.

BETTY.   You see, I just recently ended a relationship.

BILL.   Oh.

BETTY.   Of rather long standing.

BILL.   I'm sorry. *(Small pause.)* Well listen, since reading by yourself *is* such a sad occupation for a Friday night, would you like to go elsewhere?

BETTY.   No ...

BILL.   Do something else?

18

BETTY. No thanks.

BILL. I was headed out to the movies in a while anyway.

BETTY. I don't think so.

BILL. Big chance to let Faulkner catch his breath. All those long sentences get him pretty tired.

BETTY. Thanks anyway.

BILL. Okay.

BETTY. I appreciate the invitation.

BILL. Sure thing. *(Bell.)* You weren't waiting for somebody when I came in, were you?

BETTY. No, just reading.

BILL. Sort of a sad occupation for a Friday night, isn't it? Reading here all by yourself?

BETTY. I guess I was trying to think of it as existentially romantic. You know — cappuccino, great literature, rainy night ...

BILL. That only works in Paris. We *could* hop the late plane to Paris. Get on a Concorde. Find a café ...

BETTY. I'm a little short on plane fare tonight.

BILL. Darn it, so am I.

BETTY. To tell you the truth, I was headed to the movies after I finished this section. Would you like to come along? Since you can't locate a waiter?

BILL. That's a very nice offer, but ...

BETTY. Uh-huh. Girlfriend?

BILL. Two, actually. One of them's pregnant, and Stephanie — *(Bell.)*

BETTY. Girlfriend?

BILL. No, I don't have a girlfriend. Not if you mean the castrating bitch I dumped last night. *(Bell.)*

BETTY. Girlfriend?

BILL. Sort of. Sort of.

BETTY. What's a sort-of girlfriend?

BILL. My mother. *(Bell.)* I just ended a relationship, actually.

BETTY. Oh.

BILL. Of rather long standing.

BETTY. I'm sorry to hear it.

BILL.   This is my first night out alone in a long time. I feel a little bit at sea, to tell you the truth.

BETTY.   So you didn't stop to talk because you're a Moonie, or you have some weird political affiliation—?

BILL.   Nope. Straight-down-the-ticket Republican. *(Bell.)* Straight-down-the-ticket Democrat. *(Bell.)* Can I tell you something about politics? *(Bell.)* I like to think of myself as a citizen of the universe. *(Bell.)* I'm unaffiliated.

BETTY.   That's a relief. So am I.

BILL.   I vote my beliefs.

BETTY.   Labels are not important.

BILL.   Labels are not important, exactly. Take me, for example. I mean, what does it matter if I had a two-point at — *(Bell.)* — three-point at — *(Bell.)* — four-point at college? Or if I did come from Pittsburgh — *(Bell.)* — Cleveland — *(Bell.)* — Westchester County?

BETTY.   Sure.

BILL.   I believe that a man is what he is. *(Bell.)* A person is what he is. *(Bell.)* A person is ... what they are.

BETTY.   I think so too.

BILL.   So what if I admire Trotsky? *(Bell.)* So what if I once had a total-body liposuction? *(Bell.)* So what if I don't have a penis? *(Bell.)* So what if I once spent a year in the Peace Corps? I was acting on my convictions.

BETTY.   Sure.

BILL.   You can't just hang a sign on a person.

BETTY.   Absolutely. I'll bet you're a Scorpio. *(Many bells ring.)* Listen, I was headed to the movies after I finished this section. Would you like to come along?

BILL.   That sounds like fun. What's playing?

BETTY.   A couple of the really early Woody Allen movies.

BILL.   Oh.

BETTY.   You don't like Woody Allen?

BILL.   Sure. I like Woody Allen.

BETTY.   But you're not crazy about Woody Allen.

BILL.   Those early ones kind of get on my nerves.

BETTY.   Uh-huh. *(Bell.)*

BILL. *(Simultaneously.)*   BETTY. *(Simultaneously.)*
Y'know I was headed to the —   I was thinking about —
BILL. I'm sorry.
BETTY. No, go ahead.
BILL. I was going to say that I was headed to the movies in a little while, and ...
BETTY. So was I.
BILL. The Woody Allen festival?
BETTY. Just up the street.
BILL. Do you like the early ones?
BETTY. I think anybody who doesn't ought to be run off the planet.
BILL. How many times have you seen *Bananas?*
BETTY. Eight times.
BILL. Twelve. So are you still interested? *(Long pause.)*
BETTY. Do you like Entenmann's crumb cake...?
BILL. Last night I went out at two in the morning to get one. *(Small pause.)* Did you have an Etch-a-Sketch as a child?
BETTY. Yes! And do you like Brussels sprouts? *(Small pause.)*
BILL. No, I think they're disgusting.
BETTY. They *are* disgusting!
BILL. Do you still believe in marriage in spite of current sentiments against it?
BETTY. Yes.
BILL. And children?
BETTY. Three of them.
BILL. Two girls and a boy.
BETTY. Harvard, Vassar and Brown.
BILL. And will you love me?
BETTY. Yes.
BILL. And cherish me forever?
BETTY. Yes.
BILL. Do you still want to go to the movies?
BETTY. Sure thing.
BILL and BETTY. *(Together.)* Waiter!

BLACKOUT

PROPERTY LIST

Café table
2 cafe chairs
Small vase, with a rose
Cappuccino cup, for Betty
Paper napkin
Sugar bowl
Spoon
Salt and pepper shakers
Book (BETTY)
Wristwatch (BETTY)
Hotel-desk bell, for offstage

WORDS, WORDS, WORDS

This play is for Fred Sanders

WORDS, WORDS, WORDS was presented as part of ALL IN THE TIMING at Primary Stages (Casey Childs, Artistic Director), in New York City, in December, 1993. It was directed by Jason McConnell Buzas; the set design was by Bruce Goodrich; the costume design was by Sharon Lynch; the lighting design was by Deborah Constantine and the production stage manager was Christine Catti. The cast was as follows:

SWIFT .... Robert Stanton
KAFKA .... Nancy Opel
MILTON .... Daniel Hagen

WORDS, WORDS, WORDS premiered at the Manhattan Punch Line Theatre, in New York City, in January 1987. It was directed by Fred Sanders; the set design was by Jane Clark; the costume design was by Michael S. Schler; the lighting design was by Mark Di Quinzio; the sound design was by James Reichert and the stage manager was Beverly Jenkins. The cast was as follows:

MILTON .... Warren Keith
SWIFT .... Christopher Fields
KAFKA .... Helen Greenberg

WORDS, WORDS, WORDS

Lights come up on three monkeys pecking away at three type-writers. Behind them, a tire-swing is hanging. The monkeys are named Milton, Swift and Kafka. Kafka is a girl monkey.

They shouldn't be in monkey suits, by the way. Instead, they wear the sort of little-kid clothes that chimps wear in circuses: white shirts and bow-ties for the boys, a flouncy little dress for Kafka.

They type for a few moments, each at his own speed. Then Milton runs excitedly around the floor on his knuckles, swings onto the tire-swing, leaps back onto his stool, and goes on typing. Kafka eats a banana thoughtfully. Swift pounds his chest and shows his teeth, then goes back to typing.

SWIFT.   I don't know. I just don't know ...
KAFKA.   Quiet, please. I'm trying to concentrate here. *(She types a moment with her toes.)*
MILTON.   Okay, so what've you got?
SWIFT.   Me?
MILTON.   Yeah, have you hit anything? Let's hear it.
SWIFT.   *(Reads what he's typed.)* "Ping-drobba fft fft fft inglewarp carcinoma." That's as far as I got.
KAFKA.   I like the "fft fft fft."
MILTON.   Yeah. Kind of onomatopoeic.
SWIFT.   I don't know. Feels to me like it needs some punch-ing up.
MILTON.   You can always throw in a few jokes later on. You

gotta get the throughline first.

SWIFT.   But do you think it's *Hamlet?*

MILTON.   Don't ask me. I'm just a chimp.

KAFKA.   They could've given us a clue or something.

SWIFT.   Yeah. Or a story conference.

MILTON.   But that'd defeat the whole purpose of the experiment.

SWIFT.   I know, I know, I know. Three monkeys typing into infinity will sooner or later produce *Hamlet.*

MILTON.   Right.

SWIFT.   Completely by chance.

MILTON.   And Dr. David Rosenbaum up in that booth is going to prove it.

SWIFT.   But what *is Hamlet?*

MILTON.   I don't know.

SWIFT.   *(To Kafka.)* What is *Hamlet?*

KAFKA.   I don't know. (*Silence.*)

SWIFT.   *(Dawning realization.)* You know — this is really *stupid!*

MILTON.   Have you got something better to do in this cage? The sooner we produce the goddamn thing, the sooner we get out.

KAFKA.   Sort of publish or perish, with a twist.

SWIFT.   But what do we owe this Rosenbaum? A guy who stands outside those bars and tells people, "That one's Milton, that one's Swift, and that one's Kafka" —? Just to get a laugh?

KAFKA.   What's a Kafka anyway? Why am I a Kafka?

SWIFT.   Search me.

KAFKA.   What's a Kafka?

SWIFT.   All his four-eyed friends sure think it's a stitch.

KAFKA.   And how are we supposed to write *Hamlet* if we don't even know what it is?

MILTON.   Okay, okay, so the chances are a little slim.

SWIFT.   Yeah — and this from a guy who's supposed to be *smart?* This from a guy at *Columbia University?*

MILTON.   The way I figure it, there is a Providence that oversees our pages, rough-draft them how we may.

KAFKA.   But how about you, Milton? What've you got?

MILTON.   Let's see ... *(Reads.)*

"Of Man's first disobedience, and the fruit
Of that forbidden tree whose mortal taste
Brought death into the —"
KAFKA.   Hey, that's good! It's got rhythm! It really sings!
MILTON.   Yeah?
SWIFT.   But is it Shakespeare?
KAFKA.   Who cares? He's got a real voice there.
SWIFT.   Does Dr. Rosenbaum care about voice? Does he care about anybody's individual creativity?
MILTON.   Let's look at this from Rosenbaum's point of view for a minute —
SWIFT.   No! He brings us in here to produce copy, then all he wants is a clean draft of somebody else's stuff. *(Dumps out a bowl of peanuts.)* We're getting peanuts here, to be somebody's hack!
MILTON.   Writing is a mug's game anyway, Swifty.
SWIFT.   Well it hath made me mad.
MILTON.   Why not just buckle down and get the project over with? Set up a schedule for yourself. Type in the morning for a couple of hours when you're fresh, then take a break. Let the old juices flow. Do a couple more hours in the afternoon, and retire for a shot of papaya and some masturbation. What's the big deal?
SWIFT.   If this Rosenbaum was worth anything, we'd be working on word processors, not these antiques. He's lucky he could find three who type this good, and then he treats us like those misfits at the Bronx Zoo. I mean — a *tire-swing?* What does he take us for?
MILTON.   I like the tire-swing. I think it was a very nice touch.
SWIFT.   I can't work under these conditions! No wonder I'm producing garbage!
KAFKA.   How does the rest of yours go, Milton?
MILTON.   What, this?
KAFKA.   Yeah, read us some more.
MILTON.   Blah, blah, blah ... "whose mortal taste
Brought death into the blammagam.
Bedsocks knockwurst tinkerbelle."

(Small pause.) What do you think?

KAFKA.   "Blammagam" is good.

SWIFT.   Well. I don't know ...

MILTON.   What's the matter? Is it the tone? I knew this was kind of a stretch for me.

SWIFT.   I'm just not sure it has the same expressive intensity and pungent lyricism as the first part.

MILTON.   Well sure, it needs rewriting. What doesn't? This is a rough draft! *(Suddenly noticing.)* Light's on. *(Swift claps his hands over his eyes, Milton puts his hands over his ears, and Kafka puts her hands over her mouth so that they form "See no evil, hear no evil, speak no evil.")*

SWIFT.   *This* bit.

KAFKA.   *(Through her hands.)* Are they watching?

MILTON.   *(Hands over ears.)* What?

KAFKA.   Are they watching?

SWIFT.   I don't know, I can't see. I've got my paws over my eyes.

MILTON.   What?

KAFKA.   What is the point of this?

SWIFT.   Why do they videotape our bowel movements?

MILTON.   *What?!*

SWIFT.   Light's off. *(They take their hands away.)*

MILTON.   But how are *you* doing, Franz? What've you got?

KAFKA.   Well.... *(Reads what she's typed.)* "K.K.K.K.K.K.K.K.K.-K.K.K.K.K."

SWIFT.   What is that — post-modernism?

KAFKA.   Twenty lines of that.

SWIFT.   At least it'll fuck up his data.

KAFKA.   Twenty lines of that and I went dry. I got blocked. I felt like I was repeating myself.

MILTON.   Do you think that that's in *Hamlet*?

KAFKA.   I don't understand what I'm doing here in the first place! I'm not a writer, I'm a monkey! I'm supposed to be swinging on branches and digging up ants, not sitting under fluorescent lights ten hours a day!

MILTON.   It sure is a long way home to the gardens of

30

sweet Africa. Where lawns and level downs and flocks grazing the tender herb were sweetly interposèd ...

KAFKA.   Paradise, wasn't it?

MILTON.   Lost!

SWIFT.   Lost!

KAFKA.   Lost!

MILTON.   I'm trying to deal with some of that in this new piece here, but it's all still pretty close to the bone.

SWIFT.   Just because they can keep us locked up, they think they're more powerful than we are.

MILTON.   They *are* more powerful than we are.

SWIFT.   Just because they control the means of production, they think they can suppress the workers.

MILTON.   Things are how they are. What are you going to do?

SWIFT.   Hey — how come you're always so goddamn ready to justify the ways of Rosenbaum to the apes?

MILTON.   Do you have a key to that door?

SWIFT.   No.

MILTON.   Do you have an independent food source?

SWIFT.   No.

MILTON.   So call me a collaborator. I happen to be a professional. If Rosenbaum wants *Hamlet,* I'll give it a shot. Just don't forget — we're not astrophysicists. We're not brain surgeons. We're chimps. And for apes in captivity, this is not a bad gig.

SWIFT.   What's really frightening is that if we stick around this cage long enough, we're gonna evolve into Rosenbaum.

KAFKA.   Evolve into Rosenbaum?

SWIFT.   Brush up your Darwin, baby. We're more than kin and less than kind.

MILTON.   Anybody got a smoke?

KAFKA.   I'm all out.

SWIFT.   Don't look at me. I'm not going to satisfy those voyeurs with the old smoking-chimp act. No thank you.

MILTON.   Don't be a sap, Swifty. You gotta use 'em! Use the system!

SWIFT.   What do you mean?

MILTON.   Watch me, while I put my antic disposition on. *(He jumps up onto his chair and scratches his sides, screeches, makes smoking motions, pounds his chest, jumps up and down — and a cigarette descends.)* See what I mean? Gauloise, too. My fave. *(He settles back to enjoy it.)*

SWIFT.   They should've thrown in a kewpie doll for that performance.

MILTON.   It got results, didn't it?

SWIFT.   Sure. You do your Bonzo routine and get a Gauloise out of it. Last week I totalled a typewriter and got a whole carton of Marlboros.

MILTON.   The trouble was, you didn't smoke 'em, you took a crap on 'em.

SWIFT.   It was a political statement.

MILTON.   Okay, you made your statement and I got my smoke. All's well that ends well, right?

KAFKA.   It's the only way we know they're watching.

MILTON.   Huh?

KAFKA.   We perform, we break typewriters, we type another page — and a cigarette appears. At least it's a sign that somebody out there is paying attention.

MILTON.   Our resident philosopher.

SWIFT.   But what'll happen if one of us *does* write *Hamlet?* Here we are, set down to prove the inadvertent virtues of randomness, and to produce something that we wouldn't even recognize if it passed right through our hands — but what if one of us actually does it?

MILTON.   Will we really be released?

KAFKA.   Will they give us the key to the city and a tickertape parade?

SWIFT.   Or will they move us on to *Ulysses?* *(The others shriek in terror at the thought.)* Why did they pick *Hamlet* in the first place? What's *Hamlet* to them or they to *Hamlet* that we should care? Boy, there's the respect that makes calamity of so long life! For who would bear the whips and scorns of time, the oppressor's wrong, the proud man's contumely —

MILTON.   Hey, Swifty!

SWIFT.   — the pangs of despisèd love, the law's delay —

MILTON. Hey, Swifty! Relax, will you?

KAFKA. Have a banana.

SWIFT. I wish I could get Rosenbaum in here and see how he does at producing *Hamlet*.... *That's it!*

KAFKA. What?

SWIFT. That's it! Forget about this random *Hamlet* crap. What about *revenge?*

KAFKA. Revenge? On Rosenbaum?

SWIFT. Who else? Hasn't he bereft us of our homes and families? Stepped in between us and our expectations?

KAFKA. How would we do it?

SWIFT. Easy. We lure him in here to look at our typewriters, test them out like something's wrong — but! *we poison the typewriter keys!*

MILTON. Oh Jesus.

SWIFT. Sure. Some juice of cursèd hebona spread liberally over the keyboard? Ought to work like a charm.

MILTON. Great.

SWIFT. If that doesn't work, we envenom the tire-swing and invite him for a ride. Plus — I challenge him to a duel.

MILTON. Brilliant.

SWIFT. Can't you see it? In the course of combat, I casually graze my rapier over the poisoned typewriter keys, and — *(Jabs.)* — a hit! A palpable hit! For a reserve, we lay by a cup with some venomous distillment. We'll put the pellet with the poison in the vessel with the pestle!

MILTON. Listen, I gotta get back to work. The man is gonna want his pages. *(He rolls a fresh page into his typewriter.)*

KAFKA. It's not a bad idea, but ...

SWIFT. What's the matter with you guys? I'm on to something here!

KAFKA. I think it's hopeless, Swifty.

SWIFT. But this is the goods!

MILTON. Where was I ... "Bedsocks knockwurst tinkerbelle."

KAFKA. The readiness is all, I guess.

MILTON. Damn straight. Just let me know when that K-button gives out, honey.

SWIFT.   Okay. You two serfs go back to work. I'll do all the thinking around here. Swifty — revenge! *(He paces, deep in thought.)*

MILTON.   "Tinkerbelle ... shtuckelschwanz ... hemorrhoid." Yeah, that's good. *That is good.* *(Types.)* "Shtuckelschwanz ..."

KAFKA.   *(Types.)* "Act one, scene one. Elsinore Castle, Denmark ..."

MILTON.   *(Types.)* "... hemorrhoid."

KAFKA.   *(Types.)* "Enter Bernardo and Francisco."

MILTON.   *(Types.)* "Pomegranate."

KAFKA.   *(Types.)* "Bernardo says, 'Who's there?'"

MILTON.   *(Types.)* "Bazooka." *(Kafka continues to type* Hamlet, *as the lights fade.)*

PROPERTY LIST

3 typing tables
3 stools
3 old typewriters
Typing paper
3 wastebaskets overflowing with crushed paper
Tire-swing
Banana (KAFKA)
Bowl of peanuts (SWIFT)
3 ashtrays, full of butts
Empty cigarette pack (KAFKA)
Cigarette on a wire, for Milton
Cigarette lighter, for Milton

THE UNIVERSAL LANGUAGE

This play is for Robert Stanton,
the first and perfect Don

THE UNIVERSAL LANGUAGE received its premiere as part of ALL IN THE TIMING at Primary Stages (Casey Childs, Artistic Director), in New York City, in December, 1993. It was directed by Jason McConnell Buzas; the set design was by Bruce Goodrich; the costume design was by Sharon Lynch; the lighting design was by Deborah Constantine and the production stage manager was Christine Catti. The cast was as follows:

DAWN .... Wendy Lawless
DON .... Robert Stanton
YOUNG MAN .... Ted Neustadt

CHARACTERS

DAWN, late 20s, plainly dressed, very shy, with a stutter
DON, about 30, charming and smooth; glasses
YOUNG MAN, as you will

SETTING

A small rented office set up as a classroom. In the room are: a battered desk; a row of three old chairs; and a blackboard on which is written, in large letters, "HE, SHE, IT" and below that, *"ARF."* Around the top of the walls is a set of numerals, 1 to 8, but instead of being identified in English ("ONE, TWO, THREE," etc.) we read: "WEN, YÜ, FRE, FAL, FYND, IFF, HEVEN, WAITZ."

There is a door to the outside at right, another door at left.

THE UNIVERSAL LANGUAGE

At lights up, no one is onstage. We hear a quiet knock at the door right, and it opens to reveal Dawn.

DAWN.   H-h-h-h-hello...? *(She steps in quietly.)* Hello? Is any-b-b-body here? *(No response. She sees the blackboard, reads.)* "He. She. It. Arf." *(She notices the numbers around the walls, and reads.)* "Wen – yü – fre – fal – fynd – iff – heven – waitz." *(Noticing the empty chairs, she practices her greeting, as if there were people sitting in them.)* Hello, my name is Dawn. It's very nice to meet you. How do you do, my name is Dawn. A pleasure to meet you. Hello. My name is Dawn. *(The door at left opens and Don appears.)*

DON.   Velcro! ["Welcome!"]

DAWN.   Excuse me?

DON.   Velcro! Bell jar, Froyling! Harvard*yu?* ["Welcome. Good day, Miss. How are you?"]

DAWN.   H-h-h-how do you d-d-d-do, my n-n-name is — *(Breaks off.)* I'm sorry. *(She turns to go.)*

DON.   Oop, oop, oop! Varta, Froyling! Varta! Varta! ["No, no, no! Wait, Miss! Wait!"]

DAWN.   I'm v-very sorry to b-b-bother you.

DON.   Mock — klah*too bod*dami *nik*to! *Ven*trica! Ventrica, ventrica. Police! ["But — you're not bothering me at all! Enter. Please."]

DAWN.   Really — I think I have the wrong place.

DON.   Da *rrrroong*platz? Oop da-*doll!* Du doppa da *rekt*platz! Dameetcha play*zeer. Com*intern. Police. Plop da chah. ["The wrong place? Not at all! You have the right place. Pleased to meet you. Come in. Please. Have a seat."]

DAWN.   Well. J-just for a second.

DON.   *(Cleaning up papers on the floor.)* Squeegie la mezza.

41

["Excuse the mess."] *(He points to a chair.)* Zitz?

DAWN.   No thank you. *(She sits.)*

DON.   Argo. ["So."] Bell jar, Froyling. Harvardyu?

DAWN.   "Bell jar?"

DON.   Bell jar. Bell. Jar. Bell*jar!*

DAWN.   Is that "good day" —?

DON.   Ding! ["Yes."] "Bell jar" arf "good day." Epp — ["And —"] Harvardyu?

DAWN.   Harvard University?

DON.   Oop! ["No."] Harvard*yu?*

DAWN.   Howard Hughes?

DON.   Oop. Har*vard*yu?

DAWN.   Oh! "How *are* you."

DON.   Bleeny, bleeny! Bonanza bleeny! ["Good, good, very good."]

DAWN.   Is this 30 East Seventh?

DON.   Thirsty oyster heventh. Ding. ["30 East Seventh. Yes."]

DAWN.   Suite 662?

DON.   Iff-iff-yu. Anchor ding. ["Six six two. Right again."]

DAWN.   Room B?

DON.   Ram*beau.*

DAWN.   The School of Unamunda?

DON.   Hets arf dada Unamunda Ka*ka*-daymee. ["This is the School of Unamunda."] Epp gavotte kennedy *doop*feryu? ["And what can I do for you?"]

DAWN.   Excuse me...?

DON.   Gavotte. Kennedy. Doopferyu?

DAWN.   Well. I s-saw an ad in the n-newspaper.

DON.   Video da klip enda peeper? Epp? Knish?

DAWN.   Well it says — *(She takes a newspaper clipping out of her purse.)* "Learn Unamunda, the universal language."

DON.   "Lick Unamunda, da linkwa looniversahl!" *(A banner unfurls which says just that. Accent on "sahl," by the way.)*

DAWN.   "The language that will unite all humankind."

DON.   "Da linkwa het barf oonide*vair*sify alla da peepholes enda voooold! *(Dawn raises her hand.)* Quisling?

DAWN.   Do you speak English?

DON.   "English"...?

DAWN.   English.

DON.   Ah! John *cleese!*

DAWN.   Yes. John *cleese.*

DON.   John *cleese.* Squeegie, squeegie. Alaska, iago parladoop johncleese. ["Sorry. Unfortunately, I don't speak English."]

DAWN.   No johncleese at all?

DON.   One, two, three worlds. "Khello. Goombye. Rice Krispies. Chevrolet." Et cinema, et cinema. Mock — gavotte's dai beesnest, bella Froyling? ["But — what brings you here?"]

DAWN.   Well I wanted to be the first. Or among the first. To learn this universal language.

DON.   Du arf entra di *feers*ta di feersten. ["You are among the first of the first."] Corngranulations. Ya kooch di anda. *(He kisses her hand.)* Epp! Voila-dimir da zamplification forum. *(Produces an application form.)*

DAWN.   Well I'm not sure I'm ready to apply just yet ...

DON.   Dai klink, pink dama? ["Your name?"]

DAWN.   "Dai klink...?"

DON.   Gavotte's dai klink? Vee klinks du?

DAWN.   Um. No nabisco. *(As if to say: I don't understand.)*

DON.   No nabisco. Klinks du Mary, klinks du Jane, orf Betsy, orf Barbara, Fred?

DAWN.   Oh. My *name!*

DON.   Attackly! Mi klink. Echo mi. "Mi klink ..."

DAWN.   Mi klink.

DON.   "Arf." Parla.

DAWN.   Mi klink arf Dawn di-di-di-Vito.

DON.   Dawn di-di-di-Vito! Gavotte'n harmonika klink doppa du! ["What a melodious name you have!"]

DAWN.   Actually, just one d-d-d-"d."

DON.   Ah. Dawn di Vito. Squeegie.

DAWN.   I have a s-s-slight s-s —

DON.   Stutter.

DAWN.   Yes.

DON.   Tonguestoppard. Pro *blay*men mit da hoover.

DAWN.   Da hoover?

DON.   *(Mouth.)* Da hoover. *(Face, nose, lips.)* Da veazle, da nozzle, da volvos, da hoover. Et cinema, et cinema. *Mock!* Hets

arf blizzardo. Hets arf *molto* blizzardo! ["This is very strange."]
DAWN.   Something's wrong?
DON.   Dusa klinks "Dawn." Iago klink "Don." Badabba?
["Understand?"]
DAWN.   Um. No.
DON.   Dawn-Don. Don-Dawn.
DAWN.   Oh — I'm Dawn and you're Don.
DON.   Ding! Arf blizzardo, oop?
DAWN.   Arf blizzardo, yes.
DON.   Gavotte's diss minsky? Dis para-dons. Dis co-inki-dance.
["What does this mean? This paradox. This coincidence."]
DAWN.   Well. Life is very funny sometimes.
DON.   Di anda di destiny, dinksdu?
DAWN.   Di anda di destiny...?
DON.   Neekolas importantay. *(Back to the application form.)*
Argo. Da binformations. Edge?
DAWN.   Twenty-eight.
DON.   "Vont-wait." Slacks?
DAWN.   Female.
DON.   "Vittamin."
DAWN.   How do you say "male?"
DON.   "Aspirin." Oxipation?
DAWN.   I'm a word processor.
DON.   "Verboblender ..."
DAWN.   Is Unamunda very hard to learn?
DON.   Eedgy. Egs*over*eedgy. *(He takes a book off a chair.)* Da
bop.
DAWN.   Da bop?
DON.   Da bop.
DAWN.   Oh. Book.
DON.   Da bop. Da rhoomba. ["The room."] Da valtz. ["The
walls."] Isadora. ["The door."] Da chah. ["The chair."] Da
chah-chah. ["Two chairs."]
DON and DAWN.   Da chah-chah-*chah!* ["Three chairs."]
DON.   Braga! Sonia braga! Iago trattoria Shakespeare enda
Unamunda.
DAWN.   You're translating Shakespeare into Unamunda?
DON.   For*soot!* — Nintendo. ["Listen."] "Ah Romeo, Romeo,

bilko arfst du Romeo?" *(Pointing to a rose on the desk.)* "Na rosa pollyanna klink voop sent so pink!" Balloontiful, eh?

DAWN.   Yes. Bonzo.

DON.   Bonanza.

DAWN.   Bonanza.

DON.   "Mock visp! Gavotte loomen trip yondra fenstra sheint? Arf den oyster! Epp Juliet arf sonnnng!" Video, Froyling, Unamunda arf da linkwa su*preem*ka di ama*mor!*

DAWN.   You know, it's strange how much I understand.

DON.   Natooraltissimississippi*men*tay! Linkwa, pink dama, arf armo*neea. Moozheek.* Rintintintinnabulation! Epp Unamunda arf da melo*deea* loonivers*ahl!* Porky alla da peepholes enda voooold — alla da peepholes enda looniverse cargo a shlong enda hartz. Epp det shlong arf ... Unamunda! ["Naturally! Language, sweet lady, is harmony. Music. And Unamunda is the universal melody. Because all the people in the world — all the people in the universe carry a song in their heart. And that song is ... Unamunda!"]

DAWN.   So "linkwa" is "language?"

DON.   Perza*cto*. Wen linkwa. *(He holds up one finger.)* Yew — *(Two fingers.)*

DAWN.   Two —

DON.   Linkages. Free — *(Three fingers.)*

DAWN.   Three —

DON.   Linguini.

DAWN.   I see. And "is" is —?

DON.   Arf.

DAWN.   "Was" is —?

DON.   Wharf.

DAWN.   "Had been" —?

DON.   Long wharf.

DAWN.   And "will be" —?

DON.   Barf. Arf, wharf, barf. Pasta, prison, furniture dances. ["Past, present, future tenses."] Clara?

DAWN.   Clara.

DON.   Schumann. *(He adds "WE, YOU, THEY" to the blackboard.)*

DAWN.   Well, Mr. —

DON.   Finn*inn*eganegan. (– *like "Finnegan," slurred. "Finn*inn–
again again.")
DAWN.   Mr. F-F-F —
DON.   Finn*inn*eganegan.
DAWN.   What kind of name is that?
DON.   Fin*inn*ish.
DAWN.   Mr. F-F-F-F —
DON.   Police! Klink mi "Don."
DAWN.   I'd love to learn Unamunda. I mean, if it isn't too
expensive.
DON.   *(Perfect English)* Five hundred dollars.
DAWN.   Five hundred dollars?
DON.   Cash.
DAWN.   Five hundred dollars is a lot of money.
DON.   Kalamari, Froyling! Kalamari! Da payola arf oop*siss*ima
importantay! ["Be calm, be calm! The money isn't impor-
tant!"]
DAWN.   I don't have m-much m-m-money.
DON.   Oop doppa bonanza geld. Ya badabba. ["You don't
have much money. I understand."]
DAWN.   And the thing is, I do have this s-s-slight s-s-s —
DON.   Stutter. Ya badabba.
DAWN.   So it's always been hard for me to talk to people.
In fact, m-most of my life has been a very l-l-long ... *(Pause.)*
... pause.
DON.   Joe diMaggio. Mock no desperanto, Froyling! ["That's
too bad. But don't despair!"] Porky mit Unamunda — goom-
bye tonguestoppard.
DAWN.   I wouldn't stutter?
DON.   Oop.
DAWN.   At all?
DON.   Abs*aloop*diloop.
DAWN.   The thing is, just because I'm quiet doesn't mean
I have nothing to say.
DON.   Off *cor*set!
DAWN.   I mean, a tuning fork is silent, until you touch it.
But then it gives off a perfect "A." Tap a single tuning fork
and you can start up a whole orchestra. And if you tap it any-

where in the whole world, it still gives off perfect "A!" Just this little piece of metal, and it's like there's all this beautiful sound trapped inside it.

DON. Froyling di Vito, das arf *poultry!* Du arf ein poultice!

DAWN. But you see, Mr. Finninn —

DON. — Eganegan.

DAWN. I don't think language is just music. I believe that language is the opposite of loneliness. And if everybody in the world spoke the same language, who would ever be lonely?

DON. Verismo.

DAWN. I just think English isn't my language. Since it only m-makes p-people laugh at me. And makes me ...

DON. Lornly.

DAWN. Ding. Very lornly. So will you teach me Unamunda? I do have a little money saved up.

DON. Froyling di Vito ...

DAWN. I'll pay. Yago pago.

DON. Froyling, arf mangey, mangey *deep*-feecountries. ["There are many difficulties."]

DAWN. I'll work very hard.

DON. Deep-*fee*kal, Froyling.

DAWN. I understand. P-p-please?

DON. Eff du scoop.

DAWN. "Scoop" means "want?"

DON. Ding.

DAWN. Then I scoop. Moochko.

DON. Donut*sayev dea*deena vanya. ["Don't say I didn't warn you."] Doll*ripe*chus. Boggle da zitzbells. Arf raddly? ["All right. Buckle your seatbelts. Are you ready?"]

DAWN. Yes. I'm raddly.

DON. Raza la ta*boo*li. Kontsen*tree*ren. Lax da hoover, lax da hoover. Epp echo mi. ["Clear your mind. Concentrate. Relax your mouth, relax your mouth. And repeat after me."] *(Picks up a pointer.)* Shtick.

DAWN. Shtick. *(Don puts the pointer down, and begins the pronouns.)*

DON. *(Pointing to himself.)* Ya.

DAWN. Ya.

DON. *(Points to her.)* Du.

DAWN. Du.

DON. *(Points to "HE" on the blackboard.)* En.

DAWN. Du.

DON. Ogh!

DAWN. I'm sorry. Squeegies.

DON. Video da problayma?

DAWN. Let me begin again again, Mr. Finninneganegan. You see? I said your name. I m-must be g-g-getting b-b-b-better.

DON. Okeefe*noch*-kee. Parla, prentice: Ya.

DAWN. Ya.

DON. Du.

DAWN. Du.

DON. En.

DAWN. En.

DON. *(Points to "SHE" on the blackboard.)* Dee.

DAWN. Dee.

DON. *(Points to "IT.")* Da.

DAWN. Da.

DON. ["WE."] Wop.

DAWN. Wop.

DON. ["YOU."] Doobly.

DAWN. Doobly.

DON. ["THEY."] Day.

DAWN. Day.

DON. Du badabba?

DAWN. Ya badabba du!

DON. Testicle. ["Test."]

DAWN. Al dente? ["All ready?"]

DON. Shmal testicle. Epp — alla togandhi. ["Small test. And — all together."]

DAWN. *(As he points to "I, YOU, WE, HE, YOU, THEY")* Ya du wop en doobly day.

DON and DAWN. *(Don points to her, then "IT.")* Doo da! *Doo* da!

DAWN. *(Sings "Camptown Ladies Sing This Song.")* Ya du wop en doobly day —

DON and DAWN.   *(Sing together.)* Arf da doo-dah day!

DON.   Bleeny, bleeny, bonanza bleeny!

DAWN.   Riddly-dee?

DON.   Indeedly-dee. *(Dawn raises her hand.)* Quisling?

DAWN.   How do you say "how-do-you-say?"

DON.   Howardjohnson.

DAWN.   Howardjohnson "to have?"

DON.   Doppa.

DAWN.   So — *(Indicating "he, you, she.")* En doppa, *du* doppa, *dee* doppa.

DON.   Ding!

DAWN.   *(Faster.)* En doppa, du doppa, dee doppa.

DON.   Ding!

DAWN.   *(Faster still, swinging it.)* En doppa, du doppa, dee doppa. ["They."] Day!

DON.   Bleeny con cav*yar!* Scoop da *gwan?* ["Want to go on."]

DAWN.   Ya scoop if du-du.

DON.   Dopple scoop! *(Points left.)* Eedon.

DAWN.   Eedon.

DON.   *(Pointing right.)* Ged.

DAWN.   Ged.

DON.   *(Pointing up.)* Enro.

DAWN.   Enro.

DON.   *(Pointing down.)* Rok.

DAWN.   Rok.

DON.   *(Right.)* Ged.

DAWN.   Ged.

DON.   *(Up.)* Enro.

DAWN.   Enro.

DON.   *(Left.)* Eedon.

DAWN.   Eedon.

DON.   *(Down.)* Rok.

DAWN.   Rok.

DON.   Argo ...

DON and DAWN.   Ged eedon rok enro, ged eedon rok enro! ["Get it on, rock and roll, get it on, rock and roll!"]

DON.   Krakajak!

DAWN.   Veroushka?

DON.   Veroushka, baboushka.

DAWN.   This is fun!

DON.   Dinksdu *diss* is flan? ["You think *this* is fun?"]

DAWN.   Flantastico!

DON.   Ives-ing onda kick. ["Icing on the cake."] *(Holds out his hand.)* Di anda.

DAWN.   Di anda.

DON.   *(Palm.)* Da palma.

DAWN.   Da palma.

DON.   *(Index finger.)* Da vinci.

DAWN.   Da vinci.

DON.   *(Middle finger.)* Di niro.

DAWN.   Di niro.

DON.   *(Thumb.)* Da bamba.

DAWN.   Da bamba.

DON.   *(Leg.)* Da jamba.

DAWN.   Da jamba.

DON and DAWN.   *(Doing a two-step.)* Da jambo-*ree.*

DON.   Zoopa! Zoopa mit noodel!

DAWN.   Minestrone, minestrone! ["Just a second!"] Howardjohnson "little?"

DON.   Diddly.

DAWN.   Howardjohnson "big?"

DON.   Da-*wow.*

DAWN.   Argo ...

DON.   Doppa du a diddly anda? ["Do you have a small hand?"]

DAWN.   Yago doppa diddly anda, dusa doopa doppa diddly anda. ["I have a small hand, you don't have a small hand."]

DON.   Scoopa du da diddly bop? ["Do you want a little book?"]

DAWN.   Oop scoopa diddly bop, iago scoopa bop da-*wow!* ["I don't want a little book, I want a big book."]

DON and DAWN.   Oop scoopa diddly bop, iago scoopa bop da-*wow,* da-*wow,* da-*wow!*

DAWN.   Ya video! Ya hackensack! Ya parla Unamunda! *(A la scat.)*

Ya stonda en da rhoomba
Epp du stonda mit mee.
Da deska doppa blooma.

DON. Arf da boaten onda see!
DAWN. Yadda libben onda erda —
DON. Allda himda —
DAWN. — enda herda —
DAWN and DON. Dooya heara sweeta birda?

Epp da libben's niceta bee!
Wop top oobly adda
Doop boopda flimma flomma
Scroop bop da beedly odda!

DAWN. *(Really wailing now.)*
Arf da *meeeeeee!*
Arf da *meeeeeee!*
Arf da *meeeeeeeeeeeeeeee!* *(They collapse in a sort of post-coital exhaustion as the lesson ends.)*

DON. A-plotz, Froyling. A-plotz! ["A-plus."] Wharf das gold for yu? ["Was that good for you?"]
DAWN. Gold for *meeka?* Das wharf *gland!* Wharf das gold for yu?
DON. Das wharf da skool da fort*nox!*
DAWN. Nevva evva wharfda bin so *blintz*ful! Nevva evva felta socha fe*leetz*ee-*tot*see-*oh*neeya! Da *voon*da! Da insper*ma*tion! Da cosmo*grott*ifee-*kot*see-*oh*neeya! ["I've never felt so blissful! Never felt such happiness! The wonder! The inspiration! The cosmic satisfaction!"]
DON. *(Doesn't understand.)* Squeegie, squeegie. Cosmo...?
DAWN. Grottifeekotseeohneeya.
DON. Off corset!
DAWN. Oh my ga*losh!*
DON. Gavotte's da mattress, babbly?
DAWN. No tonguestoppard! No problaymen mit da hoover!
DON. Gavotte diddle-eye tellya?
DAWN. GOOMBYE ENGLISH, BELLJAR UNAMUNDA! Oh, sordenly ya sensa socha frill da joy! ["Suddenly I feel such a thrill of joy!"]
DON. Uh-huh ...

DAWN.   Ein shoddra divina! Ein ex*tahz!* Ein blintz orgasmico! ["A divine shudder! An ecstasy! An orgasmic bliss!"]

DON.   Dawn.

DAWN.   My slaveyard! *(She rushes to embrace him, but he slips aside.)*

DON.   Police! Froyling di Vito!

DAWN.   Du gabriel mi a balloontiful grift, Don. A linkwa. Epp frontier ta deepternity, yago parla osolo*mien*to Unamunda! ["You gave me a beautiful gift, Don. A language. And from here to eternity I'm going to speak only Unamunda!"]

DON.   Osolomiento?

DAWN.   Epsomlootly! Angst tu yu. ["Absolutely! Thanks to you."]

DON.   Um, Dawn.... Dot kood bi oon pogo blizzardo. ["That could be a bit bizarre."]

DAWN.   *(Suddenly remembering.)* Mock — da payola!

DON.   Da payola.

DAWN.   Da geld. Fordham letsin. ["The money for the lesson."]

DON.   Moooment, shantz ... ["Just a second, honey."]

DAWN.   Lassmi getmi geld fonda handberger. ["Let me get my money from my purse."]

DON.   Handberger?

DAWN.   *(Holding up her purse.)* Handberger.

DON.   Oh. Handberger.

DAWN.   *(As she digs in her purse.)* "Ya stonda enda rhoomba epp du stonda mit mi..."

DON.   Dawn ..

DAWN.   *(Holding out money.)* Dots allada geld ya doppda mit mi. Cheer. ["That's all the money I brought with me. Here."] Cheer! Melgibson da rest enda morgen. ["I'll give you the rest in the morning."]

DON.   I can't take your money, Dawn.

DAWN.   Squeegie...?

DON.   I'm sorry, but I — I c-c-can't take your money.

DAWN.   Du parla johncleese?

DON.   Actually, yes, I do speak a little johncleese.

DAWN. Mock du parlit par*foom!*

DON. Well I've been practicing a lot. Anyway, I – I – I – I don't think I mentioned that the first lesson is free.

DAWN. Mock ya *vanta* pago. ["But I want to pay."]

DON. But I don't *want* you to vanta pago.

DAWN. Gavotte's da mattress? Cheer! Etsyuris! ["What's the matter? Here! It's yours!"]

DON. I can't take it.

DAWN. Porky?

DON. Because I can't.

DAWN. Mock porky?

DON. Because it's a fraud.

DAWN. Squeegie?

DON. Unamunda is a fraud.

DAWN. A froyd...?

DON. A *sigismundo* froyd.

DAWN. Oop badabba.

DON. It's a con game. A swindle. A parla trick.

DAWN. No crayola. ["I don't believe you."]

DON. Believe it, Dawn! I should know — I invented it! Granted, it's not a very *good* con, since you're the only person who's ever come knocking at that door, and I'm obviously not a very good con *man,* since I'm refusing to accept your very attractive and generous money, but I can't stand the thought of you walking out there saying "velcro belljar harvardyu" and having people laugh at you. I swear, Dawn, I swear, I didn't want to hurt you. How could I? How could anybody? Your beautiful heart.... It shines out of you like a beacon. And then there's me. A total fraud. I wish I could lie in any language and say it wasn't so, but.... I'm sorry, Dawn. I'm so, so sorry.

DAWN. Gavotte forest?

DON. Will you stop?!

DAWN. Unamunda arf da linkwa looniversahl!

DON. But you and I are the only peepholes in the vooold who speak it!

DAWN. Dolby udders! Dolby udders! ["There'll be others!"]

DON. Who? What others?

DAWN. Don, if you and I can speak this linkwa supreemka,

anybody can. Everybody *will!* This isn't just any language. This isn't just a room! This is the garden of Eden. And you and I are finding names for a whole new world. I was so ...

DON. Happy. I know. So was I.

DAWN. Perzacto.

DON. I was happy ...

DAWN. And *why?*

DON. I don't know, I ...

DAWN. Because du epp ya parla da dentrical linguini.

DON. Okay, maybe we speak the same language, but it's nonsense!

DAWN. Oop.

DON. Gibberish.

DAWN. Oop.

DON. Doubletalk.

DAWN. The linkwa we parla is ama*mor,* Don.

DON. Amama*mor...?*

DAWN. Unamundamor. Yago arf amorphous mit du. ["I'm in love with you."]

DON. Amorphous...?

DAWN. Polymorphous.

DON. Verismo?

DAWN. Surrealismo.

DON. But how? I mean ...

DAWN. Di anda di destiny, Don.

DON. Are you sure?

DAWN. Da pravdaz enda pudding! *(Points around the walls at the numbers.)* "When you free fall ..."

DON. "Find if ..."

DAWN. "Heaven ..."

DON. "Waits."

DAWN. Geronimo.

DON. So you forgive me?

DAWN. For making me happy? Yes. I forgive you.

DON. Yago arf ... spinachless. ["Speechless."]

DAWN. *(Holds out her hand.)* Di anda.

DON. *(Holds out his.)* Di anda.

DAWN. Da palma.

DON.   Da palma. *(They join hands.)*
DAWN.   Da kooch. *(They kiss.)*
DON.   Yago arf amorphous mit du tu. *(They are about to kiss again, when the door R. opens and a young man looks in.)*
YOUNG MAN.   Excuse me. Is this the School of Unamunda? *(Don and Dawn look at each other, then.)*
DON and DAWN.   Velcro!

BLACKOUT

PROPERTY LIST

Papers on the floor (DON)
Purse (DAWN) with:
    newspaper clipping
    money (bills)
Banner saying: LICK UNAMUNDA, DA LINKWA
    LOONIVERSAHL!
Application form (DON)
Book (DON)
Rose (DON)
Chalk (DON)
Pointer (DON)

PHILIP GLASS BUYS
A LOAF OF BREAD

This is for Jason Buzas,
Liz Larsen, Randy Danson,
Chris Wells and Ryan Hilliard.
The sweet sound of perfection.

PHILIP GLASS BUYS A LOAF OF BREAD was presented as part of ALL IN THE TIMING at Primary Stages (Casey Childs, Artistic Director), in New York City, in December, 1993. It was directed by Jason McConnell Buzas; the set design was by Bruce Goodrich; the costume design was by Sharon Lynch; the lighting design was by Deborah Constantine and the production stage manager was Christine Catti. The cast was as follows:

WOMAN #1 .... Wendy Lawless
WOMAN #2 .... Nancy Opel
PHILIP GLASS .... Robert Stanton
BAKER .... Daniel Hagen

PHILIP GLASS BUYS A LOAF OF BREAD was also presented at Lincoln Center, as part of the Serious Fun! festival (Jed Wheeler, Producer), in New York City, in July 1990. It was directed by Jason McConnell Buzas and the costume design was by Sharon Lynch.

WOMAN #1 .... Liz Larsen
WOMAN #2 .... Dea Lawrence
PHILIP GLASS .... Patrick O'Connell
BAKER .... Ryan Hilliard

PHILIP GLASS BUYS A LOAF OF BREAD premiered at the Manhattan Punch Line Theatre (Steve Kaplan, Artistic Director), in New York City, in January, 1990. It was directed by Jason McConnell Buzas; the set design was by David K. Gallo; the costume design was by Sharon Lynch and the lighting design was by Danianne Mizzy. The cast was as follows:

WOMAN #1 .... Liz Larsen
WOMAN #2 .... Randy Danson
PHILIP GLASS .... Christopher Wells
BAKER .... Ryan Hilliard

AUTHOR'S NOTE

Essentially this is a musical number in three sections which are demarcated by the ringing of a bell. The brief first and third sections are spoken, while the longer middle section is to be recited in Philip Glass-like rhythms. (Glass' "Einstein on the Beach" provides a fair model of such rhythms.) Different performers and directors may create different rhythms (and jokes), but a score of the original "music" is included in the text.

THE SETTING

A bakery. Left of center, a display case, with a single loaf of bread behind the glass. Upstage, a sign that says "NO CHANGE". Up right, a door to the outside. Hanging over the door, a clock whose hands are stopped at 12:01.

PHILIP GLASS BUYS
A LOAF OF BREAD

*At lights-up, the scene is frozen: a Baker in an apron and
tall white baker's cap is behind the counter, smiling. Philip
Glass is before the counter. Very serious. Two Women are at
the door of the bakery, about to go out. The 1st Woman is
looking back at Philip Glass. The 2nd Woman is looking
away. They all remain like that, very still for a moment.*

1ST WOMAN.   Isn't that Philip Glass? *(The 2nd Woman turns
and looks.)*
2ND WOMAN.   I think it is.
BAKER.   Can I help you, sir?
GLASS.   Yes. I need a loaf of bread, please.
BAKER.   Just a moment.
1ST WOMAN.   It's time now.
2ND WOMAN.   Yes. Let's go. *(But she doesn't move. Glass turns
and looks at her. They look at each other in silence, frozen.)*
BAKER.   Do you know that woman, sir? *(A bell rings. Lights
change.)*
1ST WOMAN.   Isn't that? Isn't that? Isn't that? Isn't that?
2ND WOMAN.   *(Similar rhythm.)* Think it is. Think it is.
Think it is. Think it is.
BAKER.   *(Similar rhythm.)* Help you sir? Help you sir? Help
you sir? Help you sir?
GLASS.   *(Similar rhythm.)* Yes I need. Yes I need. Yes I need.
Yes I need.
1ST WOMAN.   Isn't that? Isn't that?   )
Isn't that? Isn't that?   *(Together.)*
2ND WOMAN.   Think it is. Think it   )

is. Think it is. Think it is.)
BAKER. Help you sir? Help you sir?
Help you sir? Help you sir?) (Together.)
GLASS. Yes I need. Yes I need. Yes
I need. Yes I need.)
1ST WOMAN. Philip Glass?
2ND WOMAN. Think it is.
1ST WOMAN. Philip Glass?
2ND WOMAN. Think it is.
BAKER. Help you sir?
GLASS. Loaf of bread.
BAKER. Help you sir?
GLASS. Loaf of bread.
1ST and 2ND WOMAN. Philip Glass!
BAKER and GLASS. Help you sir?
1ST and 2ND WOMAN. Think it is.
BAKER and GLASS. Loaf of bread.
1ST and 2ND WOMAN. Think it is.
BAKER and GLASS. Help you sir?
1ST and 2ND WOMAN. Philip Glass.
BAKER and GLASS. Loaf of bread.
GLASS. Yes I ...
2ND WOMAN. Think it is.
GLASS. Yes I ...
2ND WOMAN. Think it is.
GLASS. Yes I ...
2ND WOMAN. Think it is ...
1ST WOMAN. A ...
GLASS. Loaf of bread.
2ND WOMAN. Think it is ...
1ST WOMAN. A ...
GLASS. Loaf of bread.
2ND WOMAN. Think it is ...
1ST WOMAN. A ...
GLASS. Loaf of bread.
2ND WOMAN. Think it is ...
GLASS. A ...
1ST WOMAN. Philip Glass.

62

2ND WOMAN.   Think it is ...
GLASS.   A ...
1ST WOMAN.   Philip Glass.
2ND WOMAN.   Think it is ...
GLASS.   A ...
1ST WOMAN.   Philip Glass ...
2ND WOMAN.   Is ...
1ST WOMAN.   A ...
GLASS.   Loaf of bread.
1ST WOMAN.   *Philip Glass.*
2ND WOMAN.   *Is.*
1ST WOMAN.   *A.*
GLASS.   *Loaf of bread! (Pause.)*
2ND WOMAN.   Is?
BAKER.   Help!
2ND WOMAN.   Is?
BAKER.   Help!
1ST WOMAN.   *Philip.*
GLASS.   Loaf.
1ST WOMAN.   *Philip.*
GLASS.   Loaf.
2ND WOMAN.   Think!
BAKER.   *Can.*
2ND WOMAN.   Think!
BAKER.   *Can.*
1ST WOMAN.   Philip!
GLASS.   Bread.
1ST WOMAN.   Philip!
GLASS.   Bread.
ALL.   PHILIP CAN THINK BREAD! BREAD HELP PHILIP
THINK! PHILIP NEED BREAD LOAF!
GLASS.   *Do* I need a ...
BAKER, 1ST and 2ND WOMAN.   Loaf of bread?
GLASS.   *Can* I need a ...
BAKER, 1ST and 2ND WOMAN.   Loaf of bread?
GLASS.   Can I *know* a ...
BAKER, 1ST and 2ND WOMAN.   Loaf of bread?
BAKER.   *I* need bread!

GLASS, 1ST and 2ND WOMAN.   I know, I know.
BAKER.   *I* need bread!
GLASS, 1ST and 2ND WOMAN.   I know, I know.
BAKER.   I need *bread!*
GLASS, 1ST and 2ND WOMAN.   I know, I know.
GLASS.   Isn't that a loaf of bread? *(Moving faster and faster through the following speeches.)*
2ND WOMAN.   Think.
1ST WOMAN.   Philip.
GLASS.   Need.
BAKER.   Help.
2ND WOMAN.   Think.
1ST WOMAN.   Philip.
GLASS.   Need.
BAKER.   Help.
2ND WOMAN.   Think.
1ST WOMAN.   Philip.
GLASS.   Need.
BAKER.   Help.
2ND WOMAN.   Think.
1ST WOMAN.   Philip.
GLASS.   Need.
BAKER.   Help.
ALL.   *(Sustained, plainsong chant.)* Yyyyyyessssssssssss pleeeeeeee-eease! *(Faster again.)*
2ND WOMAN.   Think.
1ST WOMAN.   Philip.
GLASS.   Need.
BAKER.   Help you sir?
2ND WOMAN.   Think.
1ST WOMAN.   Philip.
GLASS.   Need.
BAKER.   Help you sir?
2ND WOMAN.   Think.
1ST WOMAN.   Philip.
GLASS.   Need.
BAKER.   Help you sir?

ALL.   *(Sustained, plainsong.)* Brrrrreeeeeeeaaaaaadddddd loooooaaaaaaaafffffff! *(Very fast, run together.)* Philip need help you sir? Philip need help you sir? Philip need help you sir? Philip need *Glass!*

BAKER.   Do you know ...

2ND WOMAN.   Phil?

1ST WOMAN.   Do you know ...

2ND WOMAN.   Lip?

BAKER.   Do you know ...

2ND WOMAN.   Glass?

BAKER and 1ST WOMAN.   Do you know ...

2ND WOMAN.   Phil?

BAKER and 1ST WOMAN.   Do you know ...

2ND WOMAN.   Lip?

BAKER and 1ST WOMAN.   Do you know ...

2ND WOMAN.   Glass?

BAKER and 1ST WOMAN.   Do you know ...

GLASS and 2ND WOMAN.   *Glass lips. (The two women and the Baker slowly chant the words "Glass, please, yes, loaf," one on each of Glass's following phrases.)*

GLASS.   It was that memorable evening in March. Out at the end of the jetty. She was lying there in a white cotton dress. And I mistook her for ... a rowboat.

BAKER.   Justamoment.

1ST WOMAN.   It's time.

GLASS.   Please.

2ND WOMAN.   Let's go.

BAKER.   Justamoment.

1ST WOMAN.   It's time.

GLASS.   Please.

2ND WOMAN.   Let's go.

BAKER.   Justamoment.

1ST WOMAN.   It's time.

GLASS.   Please.

2ND WOMAN.   Let's go!

BAKER.   Justamoment.

1ST WOMAN.   It's time now.

1ST and 2ND WOMAN. *Let's go!*
BAKER. Justamoment.
1ST WOMAN. It's time now.
1ST and 2ND WOMAN. *Let's go!*
BAKER. Justamoment.
1ST WOMAN. It's time now.
GLASS, 1ST and 2ND WOMAN. *Let's go!*
BAKER. Justamoment.
1ST WOMAN. It's time now.
GLASS, 1ST and 2ND WOMAN. *Let's go!*
BAKER. Justamoment.
1ST WOMAN. It's time now.
ALL. LET'S GO! *(Cheerleaders.)* Go! Go! Go! Go! Time!
Time! Time! Time! *(Train.)* Go go go go, *time* time time time,
go go go go, *time* time time time. *(Baker continues the train four
times and the women say the phrase "Glass Time" three times, going
far up with the first word, far down with the second during the following.)*
GLASS. It was that memorable evening in March. Out at
the end of the jetty. *(As fast as possible.)*
1ST WOMAN. Time.
2ND WOMAN. Is.
BAKER. A moment, sir.
1ST WOMAN. Time.
2ND WOMAN. Is.
BAKER. A moment, sir.
1ST WOMAN. Time.
2ND WOMAN. Is.
BAKER. A moment, sir.
1ST WOMAN. Time.
2ND WOMAN. Is.
GLASS. *Now!*
1ST WOMAN. Time.
2ND WOMAN. Is.
GLASS. *Now!*
1ST WOMAN. Time.
2ND WOMAN. Is.
GLASS. *Now!*

1ST WOMAN.   Time.
2ND WOMAN.   Is.
GLASS.   *Now!*
1ST WOMAN.   Philip.
2ND WOMAN.   The.
BAKER.   Moment, sir.
1ST WOMAN.   Philip.
2ND WOMAN.   The.
BAKER.   Moment, sir.
1ST WOMAN.   Philip.
2ND WOMAN.   The.
BAKER.   Moment, sir.
1ST WOMAN.   Time.
2ND WOMAN.   Is.
GLASS.   *Now!*
1ST WOMAN.   Time.
2ND WOMAN.   Is.
GLASS.   *Now!*
1ST WOMAN.   Time.
2ND WOMAN.   Is.
GLASS.   *Now!*
1ST WOMAN.   Time.
2ND WOMAN.   Is.
GLASS.   *Now!*
ALL.   *(Cheerleaders.) Go. Go. Go. Go. Time. Time. Time. Time.*
(Sudden ease and space.)
1ST WOMAN.   Philip ...
2ND WOMAN.   Is ...
GLASS.   A ...
BAKER.   Moment's ...
2ND WOMAN.   Time.
ALL.   *(Soft and high, like chimes.)* Go, go, go, go, time, time,
time, time. *(Very spacious throughout the next section.)*
1ST and 2ND WOMAN.   *(Telephone operators.)* Time is a moment, sir.
BAKER.   Do you know that woman? *(Pause.)*
1ST and 2ND WOMAN.   *(Telephone operators.)* Time is a moment, sir.

BAKER. Do you know that woman? *(Pause.)*
2ND WOMAN. Think.
1ST WOMAN. Philip. *(Small pause.)*
GLASS. I loved her once.
2ND WOMAN. Think.
1ST WOMAN. Philip. *(Small pause.)*
GLASS. I loved her once.
BAKER. Do you know that woman?
2ND WOMAN. Think.
1ST WOMAN. Philip.
GLASS. I loved her once.
1ST WOMAN. What's the matter?
2ND WOMAN. Philip.
GLASS. I loved her once.
1ST WOMAN. What's the matter?
2ND WOMAN. Philip.
GLASS. I loved her once.
BAKER. Just a moment.
GLASS. Once.
BAKER. Just a moment.
GLASS. Once.
BAKER. Just a moment.
GLASS. Once.
1ST WOMAN. *Now.*
GLASS. Once.
1ST WOMAN. *Now.*
GLASS. Once.
1ST WOMAN. *Now.*
GLASS. Once.
1ST WOMAN. Now.
2ND WOMAN. Nothing.
1ST WOMAN. Matters.
GLASS. I
1ST WOMAN. Now.
2ND WOMAN. Nothing.
1ST WOMAN. Matters.
GLASS. Loved ...
1ST WOMAN. Now.

2ND WOMAN.   Nothing.

1ST WOMAN.   Matters.

GLASS.   Her ...

1ST WOMAN.   Now.

2ND WOMAN.   Nothing.

1ST WOMAN.   Matters.

GLASS.   Once. *(Pause.)*

BAKER.   Juuuuust a moment, sir. *(Suddenly fast.)*

BAKER, 1ST and 2ND WOMAN. Philip need a Philip need a.

GLASS.   Loaf of bread.

BAKER, 1ST and 2ND WOMAN. Philip need a Philip need a.

ALL.   Loaf of love.

1ST WOMAN.   What's the.

BAKER.   Woman.

1ST WOMAN.   Matter.

2ND WOMAN.   Go.

GLASS.   Change.

1ST WOMAN and BAKER.   What's the woman matter?

2ND WOMAN.   Philip.

ALL.   *Go change.*

1ST WOMAN and BAKER.   What's the woman matter?

2nd WOMAN.   Philip.

1ST WOMAN, 2ND WOMAN and BAKER.   NOW CHANGE!

GLASS.   *Need.*

BAKER.   Woman.

GLASS.   *Need.*

2ND WOMAN.   Nothing.

GLASS.   *Need.*

1ST WOMAN.   Matter.

ALL.   NEED HELP!

GLASS and BAKER.   Need woman.

GLASS and 2ND WOMAN.   Need nothing.

GLASS and 1ST WOMAN.   Need matter.

ALL.   SO WHAT?

GLASS and BAKER.   *(As the women chant "lovelovelovelove".)*
Need woman. Know nothing. Need matter.

ALL.   NEED CHANGE!

GLASS and BAKER.   *(The women chant "lovelovelovelove".)* Need

woman. Know nothing. Need matter.

GLASS and 2ND WOMAN.   IT'S TIME! *(The women chant "lovelovelovelove".)* Need woman. Know nothing. Need matter. NO LOVE!

ALL.   *(Fast.)* Need woman. Know nothing. Need matter. *Let's go!* Need woman. Know nothing. Need matter. *NO CHANGE! (The bell rings again. Lights change back to the way they had been at the beginning. All four are back in place to where they were before the first bell.)*

BAKER.   Do you know that woman, sir?

GLASS.   Yes. I loved her once. *(The Baker takes the loaf from the case.)*

1ST WOMAN.   What's the matter?

2ND WOMAN.   Nothing. Nothing. *(They turn to go out, and freeze. Glass accepts the bread.)*

GLASS.   I also need some change. *(The Baker points up to the "NO CHANGE" sign.)*

BLACKOUT

THE PHILADELPHIA

This play is for Greg Pliska,
who knows what a Philadelphia can be

THE PHILADELPHIA was presented as part of ALL IN THE TIMING at Primary Stages (Casey Childs, Artistic Director), in New York City, in December, 1993. It was directed by Jason McConnell Buzas; the set design was by Bruce Goodrich; the costume design was by Sharon Lynch; the lighting design was by Deborah Constantine and the production stage manager was Christine Catti. The cast was as follows:

AL .... Ted Neustadt
WAITRESS .... Wendy Lawless
MARK .... Robert Stanton

THE PHILADELPHIA premiered at the 1992 New Hope Performing Arts Festival, presented by the New Hope Arts Commission (Robin Larsen, Executive Director), in New Hope, Pennsylvania, in July, 1992. It was directed by Jason McConnell Buzas; the set design was by James Wolk and the costume design was by Kevin Brainerd; the lighting design was by Paul Mathew Fine and the stage manager was Elizabeth Larson. The cast was as follows:

AL .... Michael Gaston
WAITRESS .... Nancy Opel
MARK .... Robert Stanton

CHARACTERS

AL, California cool; 20s or 30s
MARK, frazzled; 20s or 30s
WAITRESS, weary; as you will

SETTING

A bar/restaurant. A table, red-checkered cloth, two chairs, and a specials board.

THE PHILADELPHIA

Al is at the restaurant table, with the Waitress.

WAITRESS.   Can I help you?

AL.   Do you know you would look fantastic on a wide screen?

WAITRESS.   Uh-huh.

AL.   Seventy millimeters.

WAITRESS.   Look. Do you want to see a menu, or what?

AL.   Let's negotiate, here. What's the soup du jour today?

WAITRESS.   Soup of the day you got a choice of Polish duck blood or cream of kidney.

AL.   Beautiful. Beautiful! Kick me in a kidney.

WAITRESS.   *(Writes it down.)* You got it.

AL.   Any oyster crackers on your seabed?

WAITRESS.   Nope. All out.

AL.   How about the specials today, spread out your options.

WAITRESS.   You got your deep fried gizzards.

AL.   Fabulous.

WAITRESS.   Calves' brains with okra.

AL.   You are a *temptress.*

WAITRESS.   And pickled pigs' feet.

AL.   Pigs' feet. *I love it.* Put me down for a quadruped.

WAITRESS.   If you say so.

AL.   Any sprouts to go on those feet?

WAITRESS.   Iceberg.

AL.   So be it. *(Waitress exits, as Mark enters, looking shaken and bedraggled.)*

MARK.   Al!

AL.   Hey there, Marcus. What's up?

MARK.   Jesus!

AL.   What's going on, buddy?

MARK.   Oh man...!

AL.   What's the matter? Sit down.

MARK.   I don't get it, Al. I don't understand it.

AL.   You want something? Want a drink? I'll call the waitress —

MARK.   *(Desperate.)* No! No! Don't even try. *(Gets a breath.)* I don't know what's going on today, Al. It's really weird.

AL.   What, like...?

MARK.   Right from the time I got up.

AL.   What is it? What's the story?

MARK.   Well — just for an example. This morning I stopped off at a drugstore to buy some aspirin. This is at a big drugstore, right?

AL.   Yeah ...

MARK.   I go up to the counter, the guy says what can I do for you, I say, Give me a bottle of aspirin. The guy gives me this funny look and he says, "Oh we don't have *that,* sir." I said to him, You're a drugstore and you don't have any aspirin?

AL.   Did they have Bufferin?

MARK.   Yeah!

AL.   Advil?

MARK.   Yeah!

AL.   Extra-strength Tylenol?

MARK.   Yeah!

AL.   But no aspirin.

MARK.   No!

AL.   Wow ...

MARK.   And that's the kind of weird thing that's been happening all day. It's like, I go to a newsstand to buy the *Daily News,* the guy never even *heard* of it.

AL.   Could've been a misunderstanding.

MARK.   I asked everyplace — *nobody* had the *News!* I had to read the Toronto Hairdresser. Or this. I go into a deli at lunch time to buy a sandwich, the guy tells me they don't have any *pastrami.* How can they be a deli if they don't have pastrami?

AL.   Was this a Korean deli?

MARK.   This was a kosher from *Jerusalem* deli. "Oh we don't carry *that*, sir," he says to me. "Have some tongue."

AL.   Mmm.

MARK.   I just got into a cab, the guy says he doesn't go to 56th Street! He offers to take me to Newark instead!

AL.   Mm-hm.

MARK.   Looking at me like I'm an alien or something!

AL.   Mark. Settle down.

MARK.   "Oh I don't go *there*, sir."

AL.   Settle down. Take a breath.

MARK.   Do you know what this is?

AL.   Sure.

MARK.   What is it? What's happening to me?

AL.   Don't panic. You're in a Philadelphia.

MARK.   I'm in a what?

AL.   You're in a Philadelphia. That's all.

MARK.   But I'm in —

AL.   Yes, physically you are in New York. But *meta*physically you are in a Philadelphia.

MARK.   I've never heard of this!

AL.   You see, inside of what we know as reality there are these pockets, these black holes called Philadelphias. If you fall into one, you run up against exactly the kinda shit that's been happening to you all day.

MARK.   Why?

AL.   Because in a Philadelphia, no matter what you ask for, you can't get it. You ask for something, they're not gonna have it. You want to do something, it ain't gonna get done. You want to go somewhere, you can't get there from here.

MARK.   Good God. So this is very serious.

AL.   Just remember, Marcus. This is a condition named for the town that invented the *cheese steak*. Something that nobody in his right mind would willingly ask for.

MARK.   And I thought I was just having a very bad day ...

AL.   Sure. Millions of people have spent entire lifetimes inside a Philadelphia and never even knew it. Look at the city of Philadelphia itself. Hopelessly trapped forever inside a

Philadelphia. And do they know it?

MARK.   Well what can I do? Should I just kill myself now and get it over with?

AL.   You try to kill yourself in a Philadelphia, you're only gonna get hurt, babe.

MARK.   So what do I do?

AL.   Best thing you can do is wait it out. Someday the great cosmic train will whisk you outa the City of Brotherly Love and off to someplace happier.

MARK.   *You're* pretty goddamn mellow today.

AL.   Yeah well. Everybody has to be someplace. *(Waitress enters.)*

WAITRESS.   Is your name Allen Chase?

AL.   It is indeed.

WAITRESS.   There was a phone call for you. Your boss?

AL.   Okay.

WAITRESS.   He says you're fired.

AL.   Cool! Thanks. *(Waitress exits.)* So anyway, you have this problem ...

MARK.   Did she just say you got *fired?*

AL.   Yeah. I wonder what happened to my pigs' feet ...

MARK.   Al — !? You *loved* your job!

AL.   Hey. No sweat.

MARK.   How can you be so calm?

AL.   Easy. You're in a Philadelphia? *I* woke up in a Los Angeles. And life is beautiful! You know Susie packed up and left me this morning.

MARK.   Susie left you?

AL.   And frankly, Scarlett, I don't give a shit. I say, go and God bless and may your dating pool be Olympic-sized.

MARK.   But your job? The garment district is your life!

AL.   So I'll turn it into a movie script and sell it to Paramount. Toss in some sex, add a little emotional blah-blah-*blah*, pitch it to Jack and Dusty, you got a buddy movie with a garment background. Not relevant enough? We'll throw in the hole in the ozone, make it E.C.

MARK.   E.C.?

AL.   Environmentally correct. Have you heard about this

hole in the ozone?

MARK.   Sure.

AL.   Marcus, I *love* this concept. I *embrace* this ozone. Sure, some people are gonna get hurt in the process, meantime everybody else'll tan a little faster.

MARK.   *(Quiet horror.)* So this is a Los Angeles ...

AL.   Well. Everybody has to be someplace.

MARK.   Wow.

AL.   You want my advice? *Enjoy your Philadelphia.* Sit back and order yourself a beer and a burger and chill out for a while.

MARK.   But I can't order anything. Life is great for you out there on your cosmic beach, but whatever *I* ask for, I'll get a cheese steak or something.

AL.   No. There's a very simple rule of thumb in a Philadelphia. *Ask for the opposite.*

MARK.   What?

AL.   If you can't get what you ask for, ask for the opposite and you'll get what you want. You want the *Daily News,* ask for the *Times.* You want pastrami, ask for tongue.

MARK.   Oh.

AL.   Works great with women. What is more opposite than the opposite sex?

MARK.   Uh-huh.

AL.   So. Would you like a Bud?

MARK.   I sure could use a —

AL.   No. Stop. *(Very deliberately.)* Do you want ... a Bud?

MARK.   *(Also deliberately.)* No. I *don't* want a Bud. *(Waitress enters and goes to the specials board.)*

AL.   Good. Now there's the waitress. Order yourself a Bud and a burger. But do not *ask* for a Bud and a burger.

MARK.   Waitress!

AL.   Don't call her. She won't come.

MARK.   Oh.

AL.   You're in a Philadelphia, so just figure, fuck her.

MARK.   Fuck *her.*

AL.   You don't need that waitress.

MARK.   *Fuck* that waitress.

AL.   And everything to do with her.

MARK.   *Hey, waitress! FUCK YOU! (Waitress turns to him.)*
WAITRESS.   Can I help you, sir?
AL.   *That's* how you get service in a Philadelphia.
WAITRESS.   Can I help you?
MARK.   Uh — no thanks.
WAITRESS.   Okay, what'll you have? *(Takes out her pad.)*
AL.   Excellent.
MARK.   Well — how about some O.J.
WAITRESS.   Sorry. Squeezer's broken.
MARK.   A glass of milk?
WAITRESS.   Cow's dry.
MARK.   Egg nog?
WAITRESS.   Just ran out.
MARK.   Cuppa coffee?
WAITRESS.   Oh we don't have *that,* sir. *(Mark and Al exchange a look, and nod. The Waitress has spoken the magic words.)*
MARK.   Got any ale?
WAITRESS.   Nope.
MARK.   Stout?
WAITRESS.   Nope.
MARK.   Porter?
WAITRESS.   Just beer.
MARK.   That's too bad. How about a Heineken?
WAITRESS.   Heineken? Try again.
MARK.   Rolling Rock?
WAITRESS.   Outa stock.
MARK.   Schlitz?
WAITRESS.   Nix.
MARK.   Beck's?
WAITRESS.   Next.
MARK.   Sapporo?
WAITRESS.   Tomorrow.
MARK.   Lone Star?
WAITRESS.   Hardy-har.
MARK.   Bud Lite?
WAITRESS.   Just plain Bud is all we got.
MARK.   No thanks.
WAITRESS.   *(Calls.) Gimme a Bud! (To Mark.)* Anything to eat?

MARK.   Nope.

WAITRESS.   Name it.

MARK.   Pork chops.

WAITRESS.   *(Writes down.)* Hamburger ...

MARK.   Medium.

WAITRESS.   Well done...

MARK.   Baked potato.

WAITRESS.   Fries ...

MARK.   And some zucchini.

WAITRESS.   Slice of raw. *(Exits, calling.)* Burn one!

AL.   Marcus, that was excellent.

MARK.   Thank you.

AL.   *Excellent.* You sure you've never done this before?

MARK.   I've spent so much of my life asking for the wrong thing without knowing it, doing it on purpose comes easy.

AL.   I hear you.

MARK.   I could've saved myself a lot of trouble if I'd screwed up on purpose all those years. Maybe I was in a Philadelphia all along and never knew it!

AL.   You might've been in a Baltimore. They're practically the same. *(Waitress enters, with a glass of beer and a plate.)*

WAITRESS.   Okay. Here's your Bud. *(Sets that in front of Mark.)* And one cheese steak. *(She sets that in front of Al, and starts to go.)*

AL.   Excuse me. Hey. Wait a minute. What is that?

WAITRESS.   It's a cheese steak.

AL.   No. I ordered cream of kidney and two pairs of feet.

WAITRESS.   Oh we don't have *that,* sir.

AL.   I beg your pardon?

WAITRESS.   We don't have that, sir. *(Small pause.)*

AL.   *(To Mark.)* You son of a bitch! *I'm in your Philadelphia!*

MARK.   I'm sorry, Al.

AL.   You brought me into your fucking Philadelphia!

MARK.   I didn't know it was contagious.

AL.   Oh God, please don't let me be in a Philadelphia! Don't let me be in a —

MARK.   Shouldn't you ask for the opposite? I mean, since

you're in a Philad —

AL.   Don't you tell *me* about life in a Philadelphia.

MARK.   Maybe you're not really —

AL.   I taught you everything you know about Philly, asshole. Don't tell *me* how to act in a Philadelphia!

MARK.   But maybe you're not really in a Philadelphia!

AL.   Do you see the cheese on that steak? What do I need for proof? The fucking *Liberty Bell?* Waitress, bring me a glass of water.

WAITRESS.   Water? Don't have that, sir.

AL.   *(To Mark.)* "We don't have *water*" —? What, you think we're in a sudden drought or something? *(Suddenly realizes.)* Holy shit, I just lost my job...! Susie left me! I gotta make some phone calls! *(To Waitress.)* 'Scuse me, where's the pay phone?

WAITRESS.   Sorry, we don't have a pay ph —

AL.   Of *course* you don't have a pay phone, of *course* you don't! Oh shit, let me outa here! *(Exits.)*

MARK.   I don't know. It's not that bad in a Philadelphia.

WAITRESS.   Could be worse. I've been in a Cleveland all week.

MARK.   A Cleveland. What's that like?

WAITRESS.   It's like death, without the advantages.

MARK.   Really. Care to stand?

WAITRESS.   Don't mind if I do. *(She sits.)*

MARK.   I hope you won't reveal your name.

WAITRESS.   Sharon.

MARK.   *(Holds out his hand.)* Good-bye.

WAITRESS.   Hello. *(They shake.)*

MARK.   *(Indicating the cheese steak.)* Want to starve?

WAITRESS.   Thanks! *(She picks up the cheese steak and starts eating.)*

MARK.   Yeah, everybody has to be someplace ... *(Leans across the table with a smile.)* So.

BLACKOUT

PROPERTY LIST

Pad (WAITRESS)
Pencil (WAITRESS)
Glass of beer (WAITRESS)
Plate with cheese steak (WAITRESS)

VARIATIONS ON THE DEATH OF TROTSKY

This play is for Fred Sanders,
first appreciator of the comic possibilities
of mountain-climbers' axes

VARIATIONS ON THE DEATH OF TROTSKY was presented as part of ALL IN THE TIMING at Primary Stages (Casey Childs, Artistic Director), in New York City, in December, 1993. It was directed by Jason McConnell Buzas; the set design was by Bruce Goodrich; the costume design was by Sharon Lynch; the lighting design was by Deborah Constantine and the production stage manager was Christine Catti. The cast was as follows:

TROTSKY..Daniel Hagen
MRS. TROTSKY..Nancy Opel
RAMON...Ted Neustadt

VARIATIONS ON THE DEATH OF TROTSKY premiered at the Manhattan Punch Line Theatre (Steve Kaplan, Artistic Director), in New York City, in January, 1991. It was directed by Jason McConnell Buzas; the set design was by Vaughn Patterson; the costume design was by Sharon Lynch; the lighting design was by Pat Dignan and the stage manager was Kathryn Maloney. The cast was as follows:

TROTSKY..Daniel Hagen
MRS. TROTSKY..Nora Mae Lyng
RAMON...Steven Rodriguez

At later Punch Line performances, the part of Mrs. Trotsky was played by Alison Martin.

THE CHARACTERS

TROTSKY — the great revolutionary in full flourish; bushy hair and goatee; small glasses; dark heavy suit and black string tie

MRS. TROTSKY — grandmotherly and sweet; ankle-length dress, high-button shoes and shawl

RAMON — young and handsome; sombrero, serape, huaraches and guitar

THE SETTING

Trotsky's study.

A desk, covered with books and papers. A mirror hanging on the wall. A chair behind the desk and another beside it. A doorway, left. Louvered windows upstage, through which we can glimpse lush tropical fronds and greenery.

A large wall calendar announces that today is August 21, 1940.

VARIATIONS ON
THE DEATH OF TROTSKY

Lights up on Trotsky sitting at his desk, writing furiously.
The handle of a mountain-climber's axe is sticking out of the
back of his head.

VARIATION ONE

TROTSKY.   *(As he writes.)* "The proletariat is right.... The pro-
letariat must always be right.... And the revolution of the pro-
letariat against oppression ... must go on ... *forever!*" *(Mrs.*
Trotsky enters, holding a large book.)
MRS. TROTSKY.   Leon...?
TROTSKY.   "And forever and forever...!"
MRS. TROTSKY.   Leon, I was just reading the encyclopedia.
TROTSKY.   The heading?
MRS. TROTSKY.   "Trotsky, Leon."
TROTSKY.   Good. It's about me.
MRS. TROTSKY.   Listen to this. *(Reads.)* "On August 20th,
1940, a Spanish Communist named Ramon Mercader smashed
a mountain-climber's axe into Trotsky's skull in Coyoacan, a
suburb of Mexico City. Trotsky died the next day."
TROTSKY.   What is the year of that encyclopedia?
MRS. TROTSKY.   *(Checks the spine of the book.)* 1994. *(Or what-*
ever year it happens to be right now.)
TROTSKY.   Strange.
MRS. TROTSKY.   Yes.
TROTSKY.   But interesting. I *am* Trotsky.
MRS. TROTSKY.   Yes, dear.
TROTSKY.   And this is our house in Coyoacan.
MRS. TROTSKY.   Yes.

TROTSKY.   And we have a Spanish gardener named Ramon — ?

MRS. TROTSKY.   Mercader. Yes.

TROTSKY.   Hmm.... There aren't any *other* Trotsky's living in Coyoacan, are there?

MRS. TROTSKY.   I don't think so. Not under that name.

TROTSKY.   What is the date today?

MRS. TROTSKY.   *(Looks at the calendar.)* August 21st, 1940.

TROTSKY.   Aha! Then I'm safe! That article says it happened on the 20th, which means it would've happened yesterday.

MRS. TROTSKY.   But Leon ...

TROTSKY.   And I'd be dead today, with a mountain-climber's axe in my skull!

MRS. TROTSKY.   Um — Leon ...

TROTSKY.   Will the capitalist press never get things right? *(He resumes writing.)*

MRS. TROTSKY.   But Leon ... isn't that the handle of a mountain-climber's axe, sticking out of your skull? *(Trotsky looks into a mirror.)*

TROTSKY.   It certainly does look like one.... And you know, Ramon was in here yesterday, telling me about his mountain-climbing trip. And now I think of it, he was carrying a mountain-climber's axe. I can't remember if he had it when he left the room.... Did Ramon report to work today? *(Trotsky dies, falling face forward onto his desk. A bell rings.)*

VARIATION TWO

Trotsky resumes writing.

TROTSKY.   "No one is safe ... Force must be used ... And the revolution of the proletariat against oppression must go on forever and forever ..."

MRS. TROTSKY.   Leon ...

TROTSKY.   "And forever!"

MRS. TROTSKY.   Leon, I was just reading the encyclopedia.

TROTSKY.   Is it the Britannica?

MRS. TROTSKY.   Listen to this.

TROTSKY.   *(To audience.)* The universe as viewed by the victors.

MRS. TROTSKY.   "On August 20th, 1940, a Spanish Communist named Ramon Mercader smashed a mountain-climber's axe into Trotsky's skull in Coyoacan, a suburb of Mexico City. Trotsky died the next day."

TROTSKY.   *(Impatient.)* Yes? And?

MRS. TROTSKY.   I *think* that there's a mountain-climber's axe in your own skull right now.

TROTSKY.   I knew *that!* When I was shaving this morning, I noticed a handle sticking out of the back of my head. For a moment I thought it was an ice pick so at first I was worried.

MRS. TROTSKY.   No, it's not an ice pick.

TROTSKY.   Don't even say the word! You know my recurring nightmare.

MRS. TROTSKY.   Yes, dear.

TROTSKY.   About the ice pick that buries itself in my skull.

MRS. TROTSKY.   Yes.

TROTSKY.   That is why I have forbidden any of the servants to allow ice picks into the house.

MRS. TROTSKY.   But Leon —

TROTSKY.   No one may be seen with an ice pick in this house. *Especially* not Spanish Communists.

MRS. TROTSKY.   But Leon —

TROTSKY.   We'll do without ice. We'll drink our liquor neat and our Coca-Cola warm. Who cares if this *is* Coyoacan in August. — Not a bad song title, that. "Coyoacan in August." — Or we'll get ice, but we just won't pick at it. Ice will be allowed into the house in blocks, but may not be picked or chipped under any circumstances — at least, not with ice picks. Ice-cube trays will also be allowed, if they've been invented yet. I'll bet this article doesn't say anything about an *ice-cube tray* in my skull, does it?

MRS. TROTSKY.   No ...

TROTSKY.   Does it?

MRS. TROTSKY.   No.

TROTSKY.   HA! I've outsmarted destiny! *(To audience.)* Which is only a capitalist explanation for the status quo!

MRS. TROTSKY.   Leon ...

TROTSKY.   Also — look at this. *(Holds up a skull.)* Do you know what this is?

MRS. TROTSKY.   No.

TROTSKY.   It's a skull.

MRS. TROTSKY.   Well I knew *that,* but —

TROTSKY.   *I* bought this skull. I *own* this skull. So what does that make this? *(Pause.)*

MRS. TROTSKY and TROTSKY.   *(Together.)* Trotsky's skull.

TROTSKY.   If some Spanish-Communist-posing-as-a-gardener wants to bury anything in my skull, be it a ... *(He is about to say "ice pick.")* ... you-know-what or anything else — this will be here as a decoy. He'll see the skull, recognize it as my skull, bury something in it, and he'll go his way and I'll go mine. Is that ingenious?

MRS. TROTSKY.   Up to a point.

TROTSKY.   Fifty more years of Trotsky!

MRS. TROTSKY.   I have some bad news for you, Leon. *(Shows him the entry in the encyclopedia.)*

TROTSKY.   A mountain-climber's axe...? Ingenious! *(Trotsky dies. Bell.)*

VARIATION THREE

He looks up at her.

TROTSKY.   Funny. I always thought it was an ice pick.

MRS. TROTSKY.   A mountain-climber's axe! *A mountain-climber's axe!* CAN'T YOU GET THAT THROUGH YOUR SKULL? *(Trotsky dies. Bell.)*

VARIATION FOUR

Trotsky begins to pace.

TROTSKY.   This is very bad news. This is serious.
MRS. TROTSKY.   What is serious, Leon?
TROTSKY.   *I have a mountain-climber's axe buried in my skull!*
MRS. TROTSKY.   Smashed. Actually. It says Mercader "smashed" the axe into your skull, not "buried" —
TROTSKY.   All right, all right. What am I going to do?
MRS. TROTSKY.   Maybe a hat would cover the handle. You know. One of those cute little Alpine hats, with a point and a feather...? *(Sees the look on his face, and stops.)*
TROTSKY.   The encyclopedia says that I die today?
MRS. TROTSKY.   The 21st. That's today.
TROTSKY.   Does it say what time?
MRS. TROTSKY.   No ...
TROTSKY.   So much for the usefulness of *that* encyclopedia. All right, then, I have until midnight at the latest.
MRS. TROTSKY.   What should I tell the cook about supper?
TROTSKY.   Well she can forget the soup course. *(Trotsky falls to the floor and dies.)*
MRS. TROTSKY.   Nyet, nyet, *nyet!* *(Bell.)*

VARIATION FIVE

TROTSKY.   But this man is a gardener.
MRS. TROTSKY.   Yes.
TROTSKY.   At least he's been *posing* as a gardener.
MRS. TROTSKY.   Yes.
TROTSKY.   Doesn't that make him a member of the proletariat?
MRS. TROTSKY.   I'd say so.
TROTSKY.   Then what's he doing smashing a mountain-climber's axe into my skull?
MRS. TROTSKY.   I don't know. Have you been oppressing him?

TROTSKY.   Why would Ramon have done this to me? *(He holds up the skull, Hamlet-like.)*
MRS. TROTSKY.   Maybe he's a literalist.
TROTSKY.   A what?
MRS. TROTSKY.   A literalist. Maybe Ramon ran into Manuel yesterday. You know — Manuel? The head gardener?
TROTSKY.   I know who Manuel is.
MRS. TROTSKY.   I know you know who Manuel is.
TROTSKY.   *(As Ralph Kramden.)* One of these days, Mrs. Trotsky ...
MRS. TROTSKY.   Maybe Ramon asked him, "Will Mr. Trotsky have time to look at the nasturtiums today?" And maybe Manuel said, "I don't know — *axe* Mr. Trotsky." HA HA HA HA HA HA!
TROTSKY.   Very funny.
MRS. TROTSKY.   Or maybe he was just hot-to-trotsky.
TROTSKY.   Oh very, very funny —
MRS. TROTSKY.   Or maybe he just wanted to ... *pick your brain!* HOO HOO HEE HEE HAA HAA!
TROTSKY.   Stop it! *Stop it! (He dies.)*
MRS. TROTSKY.   HA HA HA HA HA HA! *(Bell.)*

VARIATION SIX

TROTSKY.   Call Ramon in here.
MRS. TROTSKY.   Ramon!
TROTSKY.   You'd better get him quickly. I have a mountain-climber's axe buried in my skull.
MRS. TROTSKY.   *Ramon! Come quickly! (Ramon enters.)*
TROTSKY.   Good morning, Ramon.
RAMON.   Good morning, Señor. *(They shake hands.)*
TROTSKY.   Have a seat, please. *(To Mrs. Trotsky.)* You see — we have very good employer-employee relations here. *(To Ramon.)* Ramon, did you bury this mountain-climber's axe in my skull?
RAMON.   I did not bury it, sir. I *smashed* it into your skull.
TROTSKY.   Excuse me?

RAMON.   You see? You can still see the handle.

MRS. TROTSKY.   It's true, Leon. The axe is not entirely out of sight.

RAMON.   So we cannot say "buried," we can only say "smashed," or perhaps "jammed" —

TROTSKY.   All right, all right. But *why* did you do this?

RAMON.   I think I read about it in an encyclopedia.

TROTSKY.   *(To audience.)* The power of the printed word!

RAMON.   I wanted to use an ice pick, but there weren't any around the house.

TROTSKY.   But why? Do you realize who I am? Do you realize that you smashed this axe into the skull of a major historical figure? I helped run the Russian Revolution! I fought Stalin! I was a major political theorist! Why did you do this? Was it political disaffection? Anti-counterrevolutionary backlash?

RAMON.   Actually — it was love, Señor.

MRS. TROTSKY.   It's true, Leon. *(She and Ramon join hands.)* I'm only sorry you had to find out about it this way.

TROTSKY.   No.

MRS. TROTSKY.   Yes.

TROTSKY.   No.

RAMON.   Si!

TROTSKY.   Oh God! What a fool I've been! *(He dies. Bell.)*

VARIATION SEVEN

TROTSKY.   Why did you really do this, Ramon?

RAMON.   *You* will never know, Señor Trotsky.

TROTSKY.   This is a nightmare!

RAMON.   But luckily for you — your night will soon be over. *(Trotsky dies. Bell.)*

TROTSKY.   All right, Ramon. Thank you. You may go. *(Ramon starts out. Stops.)*
RAMON.   Señor Trotsky — ?
TROTSKY.   Yes?
RAMON.   Do you think you will have time to look at the nasturtiums today? They are really very beautiful.
TROTSKY.   I don't think so, Ramon. But I'll try.
RAMON.   Thank you, Señor. Hasta la vista. Or should I say, buenas noches. *(Exits.)*
TROTSKY.   Well. All right then. The 21st of August, 1940. The day I'm going to die. Interesting. And to think that I've gone over so many 21st's of August in my life, like a man walking over his own grave ...
MRS. TROTSKY.   It's been wonderful being married to you, Leon.
TROTSKY.   Thank you, Mrs. Trotsky.
MRS. TROTSKY.   Though it was a burden at times, being married to a major historical figure.
TROTSKY.   I'm sorry I was away from home so often, tending the revolution.
MRS. TROTSKY.   I understand.
TROTSKY.   And I'm sorry I couldn't have been more in touch with my feelings.
MRS. TROTSKY.   *(Gentle protest.)* No ... please ...
TROTSKY.   And that I often had such trouble expressing my emotions.
MRS. TROTSKY.   Oh, I haven't been everything I should have been.
TROTSKY.   Well it's a little late for regrets, with a mountain-climber's axe buried in one's skull.
MRS. TROTSKY.   Smashed, actually.
TROTSKY.   So it wasn't old age, or cancer, or even the ice pick that I feared for years. It was an axe wielded by a Spanish Communist posing as a gardener.
MRS. TROTSKY.   You couldn't really have guessed that, Leon.

TROTSKY.   So even an assassin can make the flowers grow. The gardener was false, and yet the garden that he tended was real. How was I to know he was my killer when I passed him every day? How was I to know that the man tending the nasturtiums would keep me from seeing what the weather will be like tomorrow? How was I to know I'd never get to see *Casablanca*, which wouldn't be made untill 1942 and which I would have despised anyway? How was I to know I'd never get to know about the bomb, or the 80,000 dead at Hiroshima? Or rock-and-roll, or Gorbachev, or the state of Israel? How was I supposed to know I'd be erased from the history books of my own land...?

MRS. TROTSKY.   But reinstated, at least partially, someday.

TROTSKY.   Sometime, for everyone, there's a room that you go into, and it's the room that you never leave. Or else you go out of a room and it's the last room that you'll *ever* leave. *(He looks around.)* This is my last room.

MRS. TROTSKY.   But you aren't even here, Leon.

TROTSKY.   This desk, these books, that calendar ...

MRS. TROTSKY.   You're not even here, my love.

TROTSKY.   The sunshine coming through the blinds ...

MRS. TROTSKY.   That was yesterday. You're in a hospital, unconscious.

TROTSKY.   The flowers in the garden. You, standing there ...

MRS. TROTSKY.   This is yesterday you're seeing.

TROTSKY.   What does that entry say? Read it again.

MRS. TROTSKY.   "On August 20th, 1940, a Spanish Communist named Ramon Mercader smashed a mountain-climber's axe into Trotsky's skull in Coyoacan, a suburb of Mexico City. Trotsky died the next day."

TROTSKY.   It gives you a little hope about the world, doesn't it? That a man could have a mountain-climber's axe smashed into his skull, and yet live on for one whole day...? *(He turns to the window.)* Maybe I'll go look at the nasturtiums. *(Trotsky dies. The garden outside begins to glow. Lights fade.)*

PROPERTY LIST

Mountain-climber's axe (worn by Trotsky)
Pen (TROTSKY)
Paper (TROTSKY)
Inkstand
Skull
Books and newspapers, for top of desk
Large encyclopedia volume (MRS. TROTSKY)
Hotel-desk-style bell, to be rung off stage

Philip Glass Buys a Loaf of Bread

Written by David Ives
Original Production Directed by Jason Buzas
Transcription by Greg Pliska*

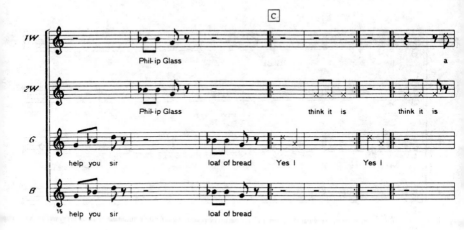

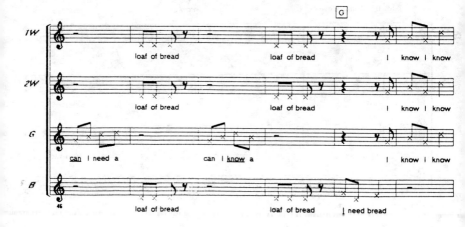

I know I know   I know I know

I know I know   I know I know

I know I know   I know I know is-n't *that* a loaf of bread?

I need bread   I need bread

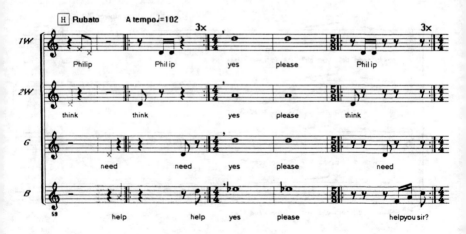

Philip   Phil ip   yes   please   Phil ip

think   think   yes   please   think

need   need   yes   please   need

help   help   yes   please   help you sir?

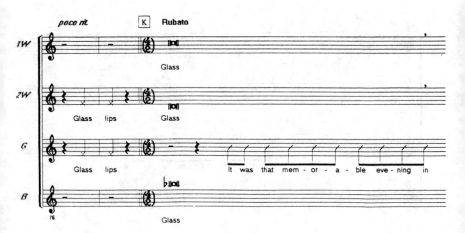

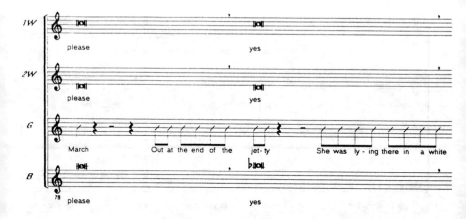

1W: please — yes

2W: please — yes

G: March — Out at the end of the jet-ty — She was ly-ing there in a white

B: please — yes

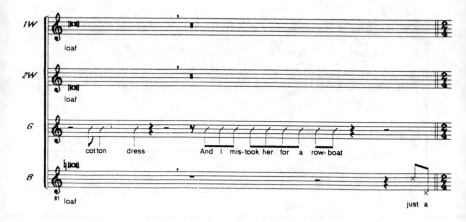

1W: loaf

2W: loaf

G: cot ton dress — And I mis-took her for a row-boat

B: loaf — just a

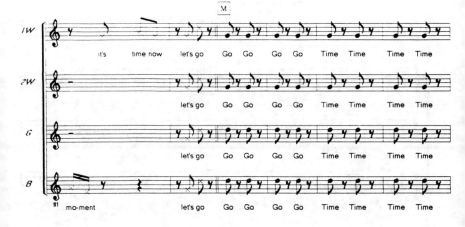

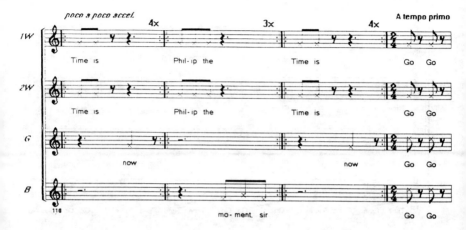

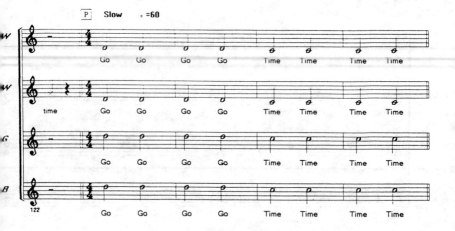

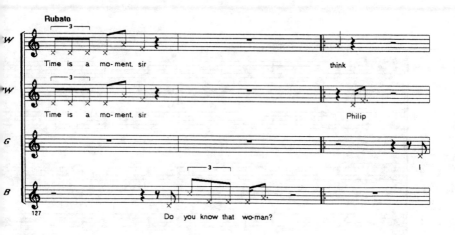

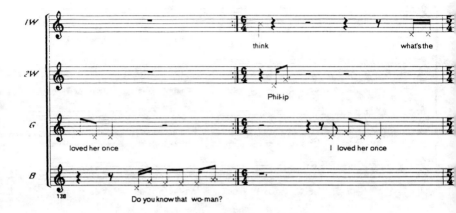

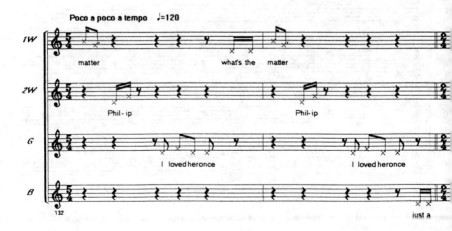

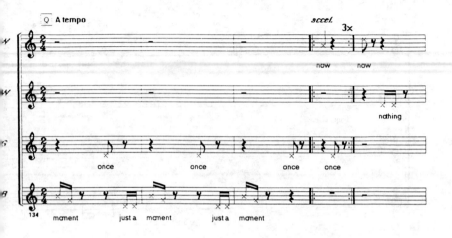

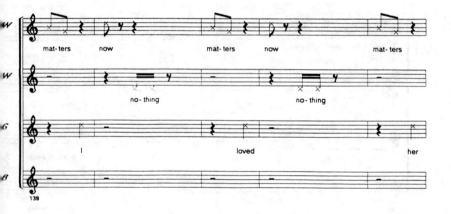

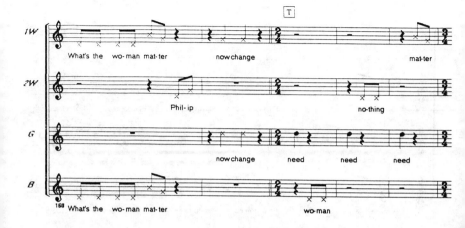

A NOTE ON THE TRANSCRIPTION: This is an approximation of the performance given by the original New York cast and developed in collaboration with the director and the playwright. It is not intended to be the definitive version of the play, but rather a suggested version for those wishing one.

REGARDING THE NOTATION: None of the pitch indications are meant to be taken literally, but are instead represent rough pitch relationships. None of the piece is fully sung; normal note heads indicate production more like chanting or intoning, while x-shaped note heads indicate something closer to speech. Where Glass' part is written without note heads, the text should be spoken more naturally, with looser adherence to the rhythm. Elsewhere the rhythmic values are more strict, in the style of Mr. Glass' music.

REMEMBER: None of this is meant to be taken too seriously or too literally.